jean-marie bub

maneater

MANEATER
Copyright © 2021 by Jean-Marie Bub. All Rights Reserved.

All rights reserved. No part of this book may be reproduced in any form or by any electronic or mechanical means including information storage and retrieval systems, without permission in writing from the author. The only exception is by a reviewer, who may quote short excerpts in a review.

Cover designed by Jean-Marie Bub
Visit my website at jeanmariebub.com
Printed in the United States of America
First Printing: Feb 2021
ISBN- 9798707833793

jean-marie bub

## and when i tell you that i'm a maneater, i mean it –

no man has ever broken me, but i have broken every man that has touched this flesh
and i have, and will continue to, shatter the bones in every hand that has attempted to pry its way into this calloused heart...
because the only one who can break me,
is me.

                    and i already broke myself a long fucking time ago.

maneater

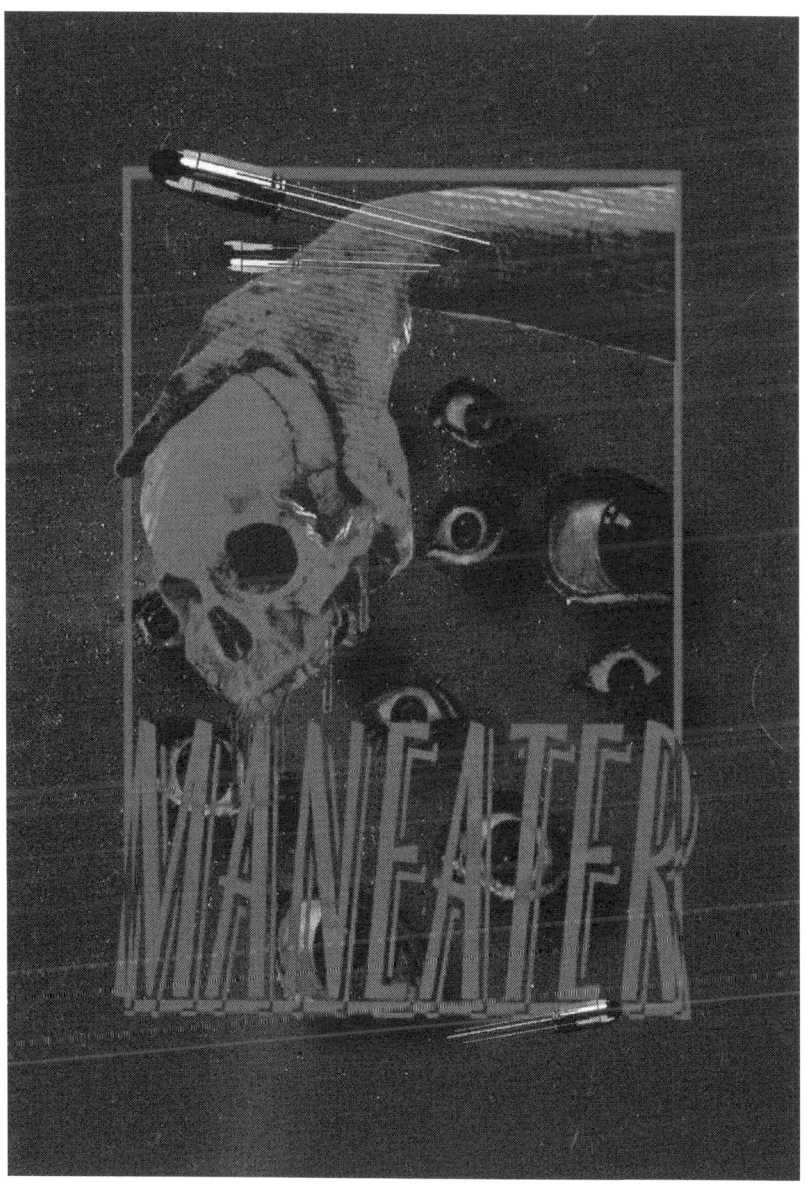

# trigger warning

This book has mentions of self-harm, rape, sexual assault and abuse. Please pace yourself when reading.

My writing is raw because I refuse to dance around truths. Some of my work may trigger you. Please reach out to me (@jeanmariebub on Instagram), a friend, or one of the hotlines listed at the end of the book if you are having dark thoughts, or just need someone to talk to.

I encourage you to tell your story. Pick up a pen, open the notes app in your phone – and write your fucking heart out.

maneater

# I have some explaining to do before you read this.

I wrote this book in pieces – before, during and after a predatory and abusive 4-year relationship. These poems were written over the course of six years, through every phase that love forced me through. These poems aren't in any specific order, but it's important that I encompass and include every version of love and every encounter with man that I've experienced. Including the bad ones. And as you're about to read... they're mostly bad. It's extremely important that you, the reader, don't absorb any fears or anxieties that I have or may convey in this book. I ask that you learn and take from my lessons, but **not to take them with you.** Take the lessons and forge your own weapon out of them – not to be wielded around at the first person you see, but to be used as precautionary measure like the pepper spray you keep in your purse. To be wielded at those who deserve it. It's also important to note that I don't support, condone or advocate violence in any form, nor do I support or condone the use of hexes. These are poems about my life, but they are *poems*. Some parts are metaphorical, some parts are very real. I would never instruct or encourage you to hurt another person.

I don't want to waste time explaining what this book is, but rather, how to read through it. Every poem was a purge, and it's usually written as guttural as it felt. As a writer, this is something I'm proud of, however, it's a level of vulnerability that even I'm still getting used to being comfortable with myself. As a survivor, it may be hard to navigate. So, I ask again that you pace yourself.

xxx

// In my life, I have felt grave pain. There were moments when I swore I would never be capable of feeling anything else. I had left myself for the wolves. starved myself, cut myself, allowed my hair to grow thin, heart to grow cold — I had given up. I forgot to water the soil that had harbored me into the ground in the first place. I forgot to tend to my leaves, I forgot how important sunlight feels on the body, and I most definitely forgot to grow towards it. Instead, I had drenched myself in the tar that is suffrage. I had weighed down my once bountiful leaves, almost causing my stem to break in two — and I learned my lesson when I nearly hit the ground. For a very long time I was ashamed of my scars. I was ashamed of everything that I had done to myself — all of the burns, the cuts, the bruises. I had thought that I deserved to cower and hide, that nobody should see the monster I've made out of myself.

MANEATER is about shedding that person. Shedding the shame. The guilt. Letting go of the blame I falsely placed upon myself, and realizing that in order to move on, I must become the *right* kind of monster. The kind that confronts the demon before it crosses threshold. The one who was hiding in me all along, begging to come out. If MANEATER lives in me, she lives in you too. The question is... are you ready to shatter the old version of yourself? Are you ready to *become*? //

xxx

maneater

writing this was an exorcism in itself.

an exorcism of the throat —
to free it's trapped ghosts.

jean-marie bub

# table of contents

i am lady Lazarus ............................................. 2

we are the sacrificial lambs ........................... 38

confronting the monster ................................. 59

loud noises and men's voices ......................... 87

for the men i've eaten .................................... 116

help resources ................................................ 156

# maneater

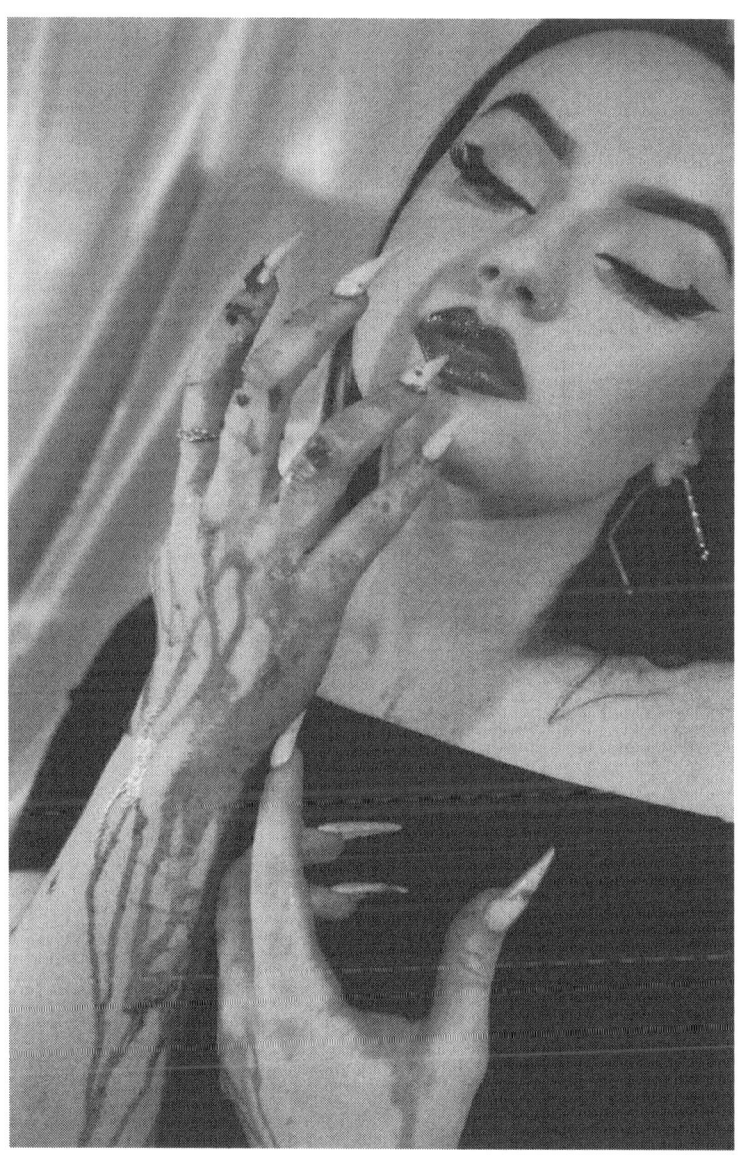

*Photo by T Gilliam*

jean-marie bub

# i am lady lazarus

"Her thirst for blood is almost palpable. Looking in her eyes, I saw the moment of my own death."

# maneater

*Photo by T Gilliam*

jean-marie bub

**wom · an**
/ˈwo͞omən/

*noun*
    a creature much too often confined

## maneater

Woman will be girl and be labeled as woman. She will have her innocence stripped from her as soon as she is brought into this world. She will have to gauge the threat of every man she encounters. Woman will be conditioned to accept violence. If not from her father, from what she watches or from what she reads. If not seen on the street, she will live through the experience of a friend. Woman will hear about it until she finally endures. It's not a matter of if, but when. And when she does, she would have already known to keep it to herself. Because no one believes women. Womanhood can be summed up in one word — trauma. Woman will be harassed. Woman will be belittled. Woman will be grabbed. Woman will be scaled down to the meat on her bones. Woman might get murdered for saying no. We all know a woman who's been raped. Woman will have to be ready to fight for her life on every corner. Woman will have to carry blade and gun and taser and it still won't be enough. Woman will have to learn how to escape chokeholds and zip ties and trunks of cars and to yell FIRE because nobody gives a fuck about a woman who's getting raped. Because yelling RAPE might invite another man to join. Because yelling RAPE might invite another man to join. BECAUSE YELLING RAPE MIGHT INVITE ANOTHER MAN TO JOIN. Read that again. Woman will have to stomach THAT pain and explain it to her daughter. Woman will have to brace for impact. Woman will be expected to spread her legs when asked. Woman shall not cry. Woman will starve herself so that she does not offend you by how much space she takes up. Woman will suffocate simply so that you are comfortable. Woman will suppress her anger and swallow the knives you throw at her. Woman will be expected to stay even after you hit her. Woman will be expected to stay after you rape her. Woman will be expected to bare and birth your child with no aid. Woman will be expected to clean up your mess with no complaint. Woman will be expected to cover up her body just to get raped for being woman. Woman will be expected to shut the fuck up. Woman will be expected to meet man's expectations regardless of how she feels. Woman will be laughed at. Woman will be mocked. Woman will hoard and store her feelings neatly in filing cabinets in the attic as to not shatter the box you put her in. Woman will be encompassed with trauma. Woman will seek help and you'll call her crazy. Woman will answer back and you'll call her crazy. Woman will ask you to please stop hurting her and you'll call her crazy. Woman will say no and you won't hear her. Woman will say no and you'll keep going. Woman will say no and you'll fuck her harder. Woman will tell you she's bleeding and you'll twist the knife. Woman will cry out to the sky because no one is on her side and you'll tell her she's delusional for calling upon gods. Woman will risk her life to have your child just for you to be a present absentee father. Woman will get cancer and you'll fuck her assigned nurse. Woman will come home after being groped on the subway and silenced at work and grazed by someone's penis in the break room and shut down by HR after complaining about ongoing sexual harassment for six months even though four other women have complained about the same man just to be gaslit by her fucking therapist and hollered at on

## maneater

outside of her apartment and you'll call her crazy when she breaks down on the kitchen floor because you couldn't do the dishes in the sink because that is a woman's job and you are man. Woman will cut and tear at her flesh to feel something and you'll think to yourself, oh no, I better leave. She's crazy. Woman will become physically ill from the pain of womanhood and you will watch. And you will contribute endlessly to her pain and suffering. And after watching woman be destroyed by man your whole life, the only thing that will go through your thick fucking skull will be — Oh my god. She's crazy.

But one day woman will wake up and will decide that she is tired of being tired. Woman will be forced to become blade and gun and taser. Woman will become threat before she is threatened. Woman will turn herself into weapon. Woman will fucking prosper against you. Woman will glare back at you when you attempt to undress her with your eyes. Woman will take the knives you lodged into her throat and plunge it straight into your heart.

jean-marie bub

my body, my hell.
my body, my hell.
my body, my hell.
my body, my hell.
my body, my hell.
my body, my hell.
my body, my hell.
my body, my hell.

maneater

MANEATER is Lady Lazarus. She is serpent, she is Medusa,
she takes blade to the throat of every Ghislaine,
She dismembers every predator, and
disembowels anyone who tries to silence her.

She is gun. She is sword. She is fire.
She is weapon. She sends hex with kiss
and death with words. She dissolves male gaze
With malice, like evil eye, she shoots
The poison back sevenfold.

the poetry that coats her lips sheds light
on truths they wish to bury. Vengeance *is* her voice,
And MANEATER lives in you.

**It's about time
you wake her.**

## BURN ME AT THE STAKE AND I'LL COME BACK SEVENFOLD

thoughts of me, slipping into your mind, sweet like wine
i'll ease you into this high – slowly.

                i'll allow you to hurt me once, maybe twice
                      if you make my knees weak, how i like
          before i'll allow this vengeance to creep up on you /
                                  unknowingly, you
                                      invited me in.

i'll turn quickly into bitter marmalade.
by the time you realized that you have been poisoned with the evocation of my existence, your bane tongue will fall.

                        steak on platter, bone in dish –

when i slip these daggers into the creases of your eyelids,
squeezing the juices out of what i once adored /

                          you will really understand --
           (because i'd have told you this in the beginning)
          (because i'd have known that you would do this)

you can only hurt me once.
burn me at the stake
and i'll come back                       sevenfold.

maneater

## KARMIC LOVER

eyes lock and the games begin,
just how long can we pretend

two catastrophic beings colliding, making mess not as nearly
beautiful as the stars, but

it's ours — tearing at each other's flesh to feed our own
loneliness, an insatiable lust and
wet mouths full of lies,

we become harbors for the toxic tendencies that
twist knife
I know exactly how it'll end —
it'll hurt to watch crash and burn,
a cataclysmic catastrophe

I dread our inevitable goodbye.

**DON'T WORRY ABOUT ME -**
I will just go on
to publish another sad book
filled with poems that ooze lemon juice into the cuts
that you etched into my flesh

and you can return to life before me—
you can char your lungs, paint them black with smoke,
maybe even green
with the leaves you held onto tighter than me

you can scar your throat, trying to yell loud enough
so that I could hear you

but as always, it will be much too late for me to notice
I will have already climbed over this
mountain, and as always, you will find out the hard way—
I tune out all loud noises that stem from men's voices.

And maybe that was why we retreated to what we knew;
to what you knew
before my wreckage,
before your force,

before defeat.

*maneater*

**AND WHEN I LEAVE,** I will strip you of all the color that I've introduced you to over the duration of our love. When I leave — you will feel lost. Like child in forest, man faced with his own defeat — and like a deer in headlights, you'd have to have known that the end was soon to come. But in the beginning, oh, in the beginning... I would have come to you flourishing, full of life, despite my predisposition to hate... I will come to you glorious, bountiful, and innocent, with eyes that would put the Virgin Mary to shame... but in the end, I will leave you bland. Lifeless. Defenseless. I will be full of deceit, searching to fill the voids that you created. Sprung off faithlessness, I will leave you reckless.

One by one I will pluck all the influence from your skull that I had lent to you in the beginning. I'll leave you wishing we were back to the beginning.

You will ask me to leave a couple of my plants behind, and I will. And no matter how much you water them or how much you tend to their leaves — they will wilt and die. It is only I that replenishes their want for life. And this moment, you will realize that you've become Judas. One by one I will strip my paintings from your walls, leaving them bare, leaving you naked, forcing you to endure the same emptiness you instilled within me forcing you to come face to face with your worst fear, losing me. For what is life without a muse? Without a home? Without heart? But a fear you wouldn't know you'd develop will come to light only after I leave — you will be left with nothing but the pillow you rest your head on, the same one you had, since the beginning.

Your worst fear — I will
take everything.

jean-marie bub

the hair grows back
and the wounds scab over
and the bruises fade away
and the skin mends self
and the war ends
and the rain ceases
and the river flows
and the plants grow
and life does indeed go on,

but the heart –

**the heart
grows cold**

**I SHED MY SKIN
LIKE THE SERPENT,**

born again
amongst tall grass.
I melt the soot that's been left behind
by careless lives
onto my skin... into my palms,
letting it ooze down my arms.
the pain has long gone, and past
but there's promises to be kept —

i bathe in it to get familiar
with death.

to curse the negligent
with the burden
of a scourged, bane
tongue.

i molt out of who i was
yesterday, and
today
i am born anew.

i shed my skin
like the serpent;
hurt me, baby —
and every
single
time

it'll be
shame
on
you.

Our **bodies** never really let go of the trauma. We may think we've healed; we think we've repressed it all so well until it's forgotten. We go days and months and years with no recollection of the past - whether that's reality, or lies that we feed to ourselves to survive, is your truth and your truth only to know. But we go on as long as we can before it's brought back up — something a lover says that reminds you of your last, a touch in the spot that you thought was healed from its last bouts of aches, an unexpected jolt that sends unwarranted chills down your spine - something as minuscule as her perfume - sends you all back.

Our bodies never really let go of the trauma. We just convince ourselves that it has.

every wound is a death of sorts
every wound is a death of sorts
every wound is a death of sorts
every wound is a death of sorts
every wound is a death of sorts
every wound is a death of sorts
every wound is a death of sorts
every wound is a death of sorts
every wound is a death of sorts
every wound is a death of sorts

can you see it?
when you look at me, i mean.
does it glare at you,
in all its disgusting glory?

the trauma. is it obvious?
do I carry myself
as if I'm hurt?
or do I just look mean,
scorned, since birth?

I imagine myself as a woman with **eyes for skin**
pupils darting
back and forth
dodging glances
in avoidance,
in defense.

can you hear it?
in my voice
when it trembles
when words like "fuck" melt in mouth
like butter?
when i throw these words on you
like thorns?

is it obvious?

# maneater

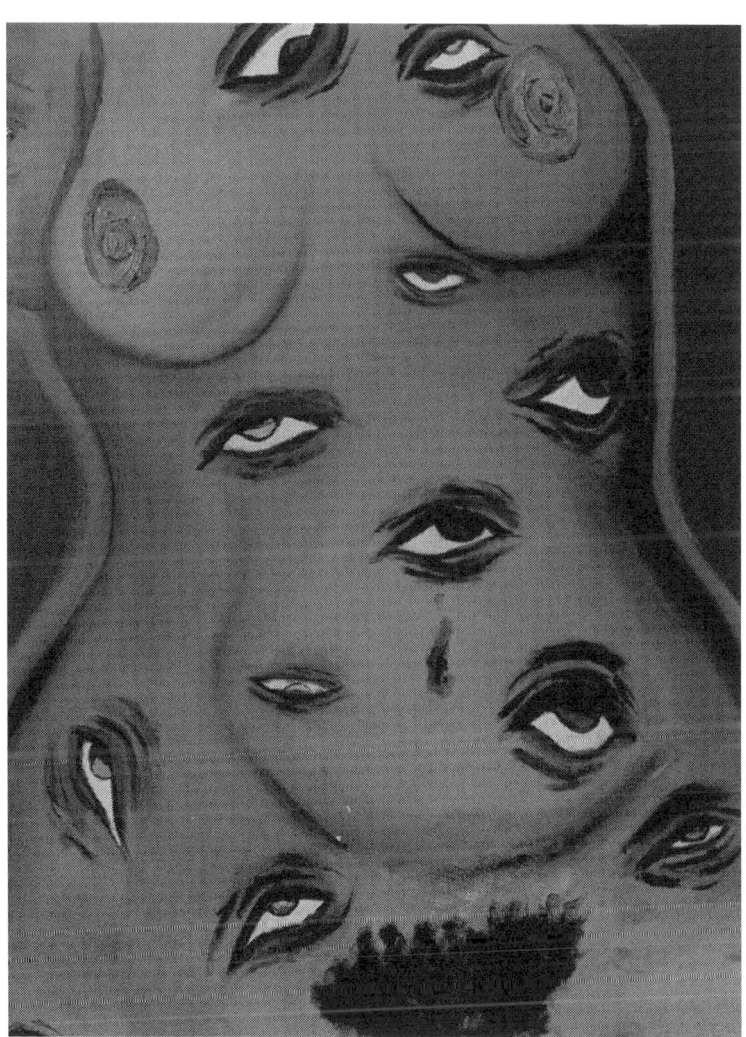

*eyes for skin, 2020*

### jean-marie bub

you tell me i'm as cold as the city. so i move there. maybe to feel something. maybe to feel nothing. and everyone there is as cold as me.

no one blinks when i cry on the train.

maneater

**BORN IN A BLIZZARD,** forced out my mother's womb Cut into this earth so brutally, how could you assume That I would be soft, or warm? I mean, I can see why my exterior would deceive you, it's a mixture of harsh beauty, and the ignorance of the male gaze, you seem to have taken my cold demeanor the wrong way, but... it's not a front, these full, round cheeks matched with this structure, with eyes like daggers that could cut through teeth, and a glare that's too good to be true, it sounds like the perfect fable, the perfect devil, you'd assume I'd be lying if I told you all that I've been through...

But one thing about me -- I'm practically married to pain. This body has been torn. I am destitute. Scorned. I've danced with death - this beauty is a two-way mirror, and you are only looking at one me. I was born cold. Freezing.

if I refused to turn over in the womb, what makes you think I'd ever fucking turn over for you?

jean-marie bub

& i'm okay with being cold. my warmth was never for you.

maneater

## I DON'T WANT TO LOOK BEAUTIFUL
i don't chisel my cheekbones out my face with paint
to look beautiful -

they sell these mascaras and
palettes at every corner
store,
i used to want to look
beautiful but
i don't want that anymore.
beautiful is too easy to
achieve nowadays
my bone structure wasn't
made to cascade
down the frown lines of my
face, my forehead plateau's
for miles
and you will NEVER see
me smile
over adjectives, please...

value doesn't stem from
your genetic lottery
you cultivate it from
within
how are you gonna
compliment me for
something i didn't have
to work for to win?

i rather be anything
than just
beautiful.
**(at least haunting lingers)**

maneater

jean-marie bub

i smell like cherry merlot, with angel dipped hips and
lips of satin, tell me I'm not the perfect monstress
that'll devour you from within

Lady Lazarus in the flesh
this will be your first and last
dance with death

underestimate any woman and it'll be you
that pays the ultimate consequence.

maneater

jean-marie bub

do i want to be loved

    or do i want to be ravished?

        i think i'd rather be gouged

## maneater

When I was younger, Bukowski entranced me.

Men gave flowers as hush money and used affection as bargaining chip in exchange for my silence. I thought love had to be like this.

Bukowski's words stained the insides of my mouth like my his did. Violent and kicking,
I thought love had to be like this —
Like it should kill you. Like you should love him
Until he kills you.

Like the cigarette that falls daintily from mouth
and bottle that seductively hangs from hand, men like Bukowski romanticize abuse — they litter the world with their baggage, making monsters out of women
Making shells out of themselves.

You could almost pity them, until you realize that statistics show he probably will kill you anyway.

Bukowski lied.
There was no bluebird in my chest
I was bluebird in his cage.

**WHEN YOU BECOME A WRITER,**
they either want to hear everything
or nothing
at all.
they'll stick their squalid hands inside your mouth
only to mutilate your tongue
with interrogation
accusation and pity,
they'll want to hear your story just
one
more
time, as if putting it on paper wasn't
a grueling sacrifice of the mind...
suddenly, every single detail
no longer belongs to you, no --
it becomes theirs
they claim your words as their own
they will take your suffering and brand themselves
with the very pain you were trying to
free yourself from.
they'll remind you that you're okay this time,
that this time you made it out alive
you're okay, right?
what could possibly be wrong this time?
you wrote about it
it's over now
right?
they'll become sick of you
regurgitating the same old feelings,
they'll tell you
to write about something else --
as if you're in control of this beast
they'll even take a picture of your hurt
and make it their wallpaper on their phone --

## maneater

remember when you wanted
to kill yourself?
remember those feelings?
remember all the blood
all the hate
the tears...
can you remember how intense you felt?
when you were gasping for air in the bathroom
and you could've sworn your lungs had collapsed
within your ribcage
and sank far down into your stomach?
can you remember that heaviness?
the heaviness that you woke up to
every morning
KNOWING
that you couldn't bear to set your feet on the ground
any longer
KNOWING
that you rather be floating
with the dust mites,
on a bookshelf probably --
can you remember the heaviness?
all of that
for it to be belittled into mediocrity?
when you
become a writer
all that you ever had felt will no longer be yours.
they'll take your words

they'll take your pain
they'll take everything
and leave you with nothing
nothing but a distant memory of how things used to
be...

before all of this.

### maneater

### *in collaboration with Lyn Patterson*

scroll / scroll / like / like / empty images and filtered pictures bury life's truths.
come for the escapism, stay for the delusions
scroll / scroll / scroll / like / like / like / follow…

poets who post bullshit like "I Listen To Birds In The Woods And This Is What They Tell Me"

DISCLAIMER, ITS NOTHING
GOOD

yet there they go — follow / like / follow / like
feed my void with false hope! scroll scroll scr — *vulnerable post* and
the matrix has been broken / she's been interrupted, and how dare they!

becky drops her iphone

becky is / the bookstagrammer / the instapoet / or even the influencer, whose decided black –
is the new black so she'll… follow / follow / like / and swipe
until Black death is no longer trending on her timeline / no discernment /
just microaggressions turned internet obsession

gullible, watchful eye, false prophet, she is Amerikkka — a safe space for
internalized misogyny / she'll follow / follow / like / like the post of a victim
of rape, until case gets dropped due to crooked cops / then she'll question
the posters intent / again, no discernment / just jealous eyes fake supporting for likes –

becky, how dare you criticize me for expressing vulnerability, implying that it's somehow crass,
if being happy is in then— I'D LIKE TO MOVE THE FUCK OUT

how edgy you are, dismissing pain in the middle of pandemic- how fucking miserable you must be to mock other's looking for communities to make it through their misery / and even with carcass draped over my little fucking soapbox / and with bloodied hands clutching a razor and the bottle of pills prescribed by my therapist, I would have still lived a life more fulfilling and authentic than you—

EVEN WITH THIS TRAUMA

scroll / scroll / like / like / like. no amount of simple line dashes as lazy literary devices or ill…thought-out metaphors could shame this voice into silence / becky you —will not only consume my trauma when its trending but

I can either shove it down throat or you can keep on moving your privileged apathetic fingers—
scroll / scroll / scroll / like / like / like


unfollow.

maneater

Bloodied hands and all this trauma
Bloodied hands and all this trauma
Bloodied hands and all this trauma

Bloodied hands and all this trauma
Bloodied hands and all this trauma
Bloodied hands and all this trauma

jean-marie bub

What the fuck am I supposed to do when the only answer was you? When even my stars have conflict? When my Venus is at war with my Mars, when my sun wants to annihilate my moon? What am I supposed to do with no guidance? What do *you* suppose I do? Who'd want to mentor the monster? Who'd want this carcass indebted in sun? a walking burden, what am I supposed to do with this lack of luck, this lack of love, what do you suppose I do with all this baggage? May I rest it here?

maneater

| Zodiac : Tropical | | | | | Placidus Orb : 0 | | |
|---|---|---|---|---|---|---|---|
| ☉ | Sun | ♑ | Capricorn | 29°00' | I ASC | ♊ Gemini | 17°47' |
| ☾ | Moon | ♋ | Cancer | 9°12' | II | ♋ Cancer | 9°00' |
| ☿ | Mercury | ♒ | Aquarius | 1°27' | III | ♋ Cancer | 29°26' |
| ♀ | Venus | ♐ | Sagittarius | 23°49' | IV | ♌ Leo | 23°05' |
| ♂ | Mars | ♓ | Pisces | 12°08' | V | ♍ Virgo | 24°19' |
| ♃ | Jupiter | ♈ | Aries | 26°33' | VI | ♏ Scorpio | 5°36' |
| ♄ | Saturn | ♉ | Taurus | 10°20' | VII | ♐ Sagittarius | 17°47' |
| ♅ | Uranus | ♒ | Aquarius | 15°48' | VIII | ♑ Capricorn | 9°00' |
| ♆ | Neptune | ♒ | Aquarius | 3°54' | IX | ♑ Capricorn | 29°26' |
| ♇ | Pluto | ♐ | Sagittarius | 11°58' | X MC | ♒ Aquarius | 23°05' |
| ⚸ | Lilith | ♐ | Sagittarius | 25°23' | XI | ♓ Pisces | 24°19' |
| ☊ | N Node | ♌ | Leo | 3°47' | XII | ♉ Taurus | 5°36' |

jean-marie bub

# we are the sacrificial lambs

*"we are alone. no matter what they tell you, we women are always alone."*

maneater

where

                                          do

i

put

                                                                                     my eyes

in a train car
filled with men

   g      l      a      r      i      n      g

   at                                                                     my
thighs?

***T H R O U G H        H   I   M***

young girls walk to the bus stop
they have a whopping tablespoon of
innocence
in their pocket.

waiting on the curb by the fresh, dewy grass
an old man creeps up
brushing past their skirts, giggling
they feel bad for him.

young girls listen to what mama tells them.
their skirts are trimmed just above the knee,
sneakers shined and white.

after school, young girls ride their bikes
to the corner store.
they crave some Arizona's
gum
potato chips and lipstick.

the man at the counter asks
why they're by themselves.
they hadn't noticed.
they thought they were traveling in a pack.
confused, the five young girls
reach into their pockets
digging past the innocence to reach for their coins

## maneater

another man standing in line behind them laughs

"lipstick? sheesh. how old are y'all?"
he shakes his head.
"I never want a daughter"
the cashier laughs, winking at the girls as they hand him their cash.

young girls ride their bikes home
bellies full of iced tea
lips coated in pink
horns honk as they pass intersections —

they all
begin to notice.

## — INTRODUCTION TO WOMANHOOD

It is man (men) who is unhinged. It is he who uses darkness as a cloak to capture women, leaving them bloodied and in pieces because she refuses a date. It is he who is irrational. He sets the standard, but only for you to follow. You must remain loyal as he lies and cheats and fucks. He'll stalk you after you break up. Walking into your house unannounced. Combing through your phone and breaking into cars, killing you in your sleep for moving on. He *is* the psycho ex. "A South Carolina Woman Told Her Ex-Boyfriend She Moved On. He Responded By Killing Her And Her Two Daughters" is a real headline, but somehow it is always us that are villain in every man's story. It is man who is overly-emotional, it is he who believes he is entitled to a response after berating woman on the street. Man views it as game while we flee for our lives, clutching onto the pepper spray our mothers passed down to us. It is he who is psychopath and manipulator and control freak, monitoring what we wear and isolating us for means of power. It is he who is monster. How is it that almost all of us have been raped or assaulted but no one can pinpoint the rapist? If it's not employer it's someone's older brother and if it's not him its doctor or the lawyer on your rape case. Remember this when they claim that they're not "all the same." If he's not rapist himself, he's protecting one and if he's not protecting one, he's enabling one with his silence. We are born paranoid, restricted, and told to stay away, maimed as overreacting or dramatic but it's always our blood stains on pavement or suitcase. It is man who is delusional. Man will tell you how to love yourself, but they cannot begin to fathom the destitution that they have

## maneater

forced upon us. It is he who views us as meat and sells us into slavery as a product of lust. It is he who has cut our tongues and burned us at the stake for opening a fucking book.

It is man who is the monster, and we are forced to live in his projection.

jean-marie bub

# more real headlines

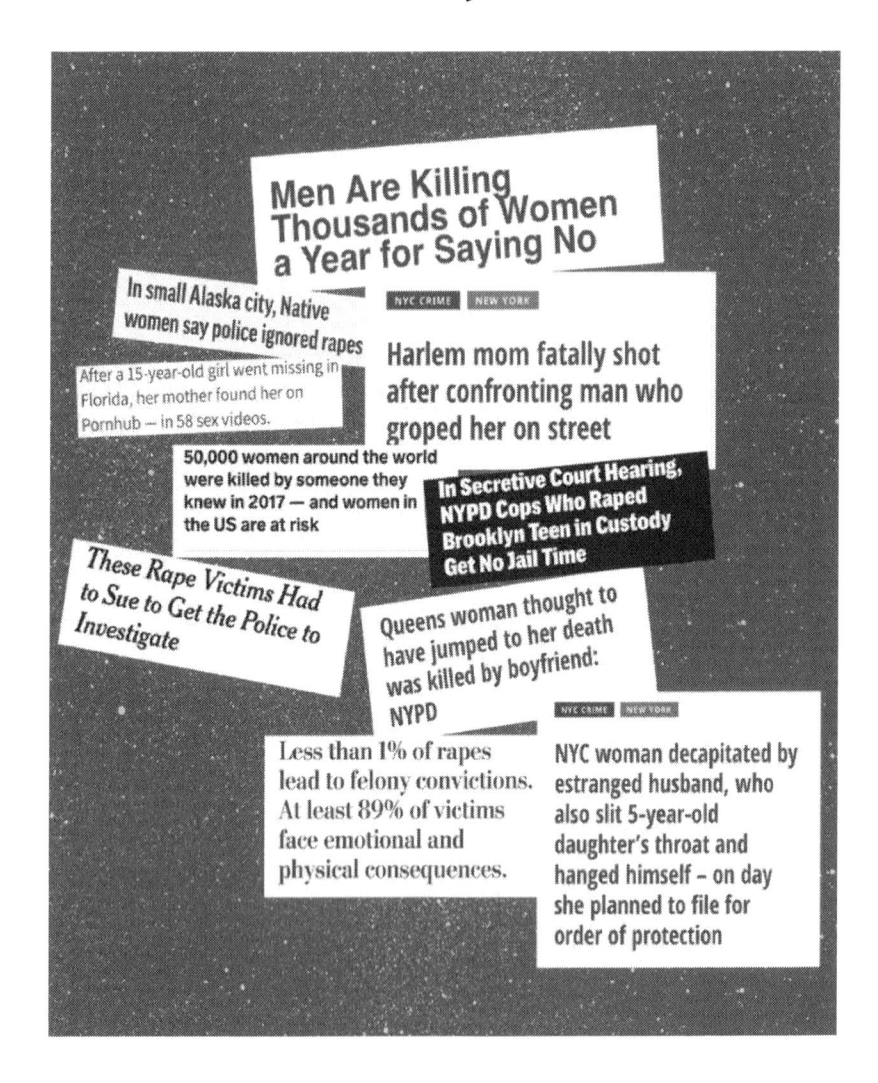

**Men Are Killing Thousands of Women a Year for Saying No**

In small Alaska city, Native women say police ignored rapes

NYC CRIME | NEW YORK
**Harlem mom fatally shot after confronting man who groped her on street**

After a 15-year-old girl went missing in Florida, her mother found her on Pornhub — in 58 sex videos.

50,000 women around the world were killed by someone they knew in 2017 — and women in the US are at risk

**In Secretive Court Hearing, NYPD Cops Who Raped Brooklyn Teen in Custody Get No Jail Time**

These Rape Victims Had to Sue to Get the Police to Investigate

**Queens woman thought to have jumped to her death was killed by boyfriend: NYPD**

Less than 1% of rapes lead to felony convictions. At least 89% of victims face emotional and physical consequences.

NYC CRIME | NEW YORK
**NYC woman decapitated by estranged husband, who also slit 5-year-old daughter's throat and hanged himself – on day she planned to file for order of protection**

maneater

### bitches always eat the bullets
when its your beef, its our bodies that lay splattered in the streets
bitches always eat the bullets
you rapped along w/ biggie he said "beef is when your moms
ain't safe up in the streets," and... hi. hello.

we are the bitches. the moms. the daughters. the sacrificial lambs
that go to the slaughter to rectify beef that wasn't even ours to
begin with. nobody ever fucking told eve about the apple. yet,
*we bitches* always eat the fucking bullets.

that's our fucking beef.

The irony of me writing this book and me surviving an attempted assault just one week prior to publishing. The irony of it not being ironic at all. Survivors are survivors are survivors are survivors. Ask me what it's like to be a woman and I will explain it to you like this. I had to interrupt myself from processing one traumatic experience to now process this one.

A couple of days prior to my attempted assault, a woman was violently assaulted not too far from where I live for politely turning down a man's advance. His advance? Wanting to buy her a bottle of wine. Her response? No thank you I appreciate it. His response? Beating her broken on the sidewalk outside while she pleads to let her go because she on her way to go pick up her daughter. The day before my attempted assault I posted about that incident only for me to come within 5 seconds of it the next day. When "hey beautiful" turns into "let me take a picture of you" turns into man pushing his way into your friend's apartment building turns into if-my-friend-didn't-buzz-me-in-when-he-did-that-man-would've-grabbed-me-and-raped-me-right-there, what do we do? 911 tells us they'll see if anyone recognizes him. They don't ask if I'm okay. They don't fucking do a thing for me. People on the street don't intervene when they see women being harassed. It's "just a compliment" until I'm face down in a fucking dumpster. The irony in me thinking that after I publish this book I can "finally heal" – in a world that will remain unchanged and just as cold. It will never be over for us. As much as we can refuse to accept such treatment, as many weapons we can carry, as many lines of defense that we may think we have, the truth fucking is – it will never be over for us. Two days after the attempted assault,

## maneater

a news story broke, again in my area. HARLEM MOM FATALLY SHOT AFTER CONFRONTING MAN WHO GROPED HER ON STREET. So it begs the question - where the fuck do we go from here?

Life does not wait for you to heal to hurt again.

.

survivors are survivors are survivors
survivors are survivors are survivors
survivors are survivors are survivors
survivors are survivors are survivors
survivors are survivors are survivors
survivors are survivors are survivors
survivors are survivors are survivors
survivors are survivors are survivors
survivors are survivors are survivors
survivors are survivors are survivors
survivors are survivors are survivors
survivors are survivors are survivors
survivors are survivors are survivors
survivors are survivors are survivors
survivors are survivors are survivors
survivors are survivors are survivors
survivors are survivors are survivors
survivors are survivors are survivors

maneater

nobody told eve
about the apple —

yet
she bares the weight
of an entire universe
worth of sin,

just as those who've come
before and after us
will have done
in the end.

## jean-marie bub

Humanity is harbored in the torso, but the torso is also the most targeted and coveted part of the female body. From our breasts, bellies and genitalia nurture the children and future of this entire planet – yet these parts have been sexualized, fetishized, and brutalized since the beginning of time. We look at these parts of ourselves every day, as exactly that – parts. But they're a part of a collective whole that deserves to exist in peace, without derogatory terms attached, without expectation of having to harbor humanity in the first place, without negative or sexual connotation, without stigma.

maneater

if the pain
that a woman bares
is far too
foreign
for your comprehension,

then you shall have
no say
in what happens
to her womb.
her bleeding body
is not your battleground,

and there is no debate —
she who harbors humanity
should control her own fate.

## jean-marie bub

What's so interesting about a broken woman? What keeps you leeches coming? Can you smell the blood? Do you wish to syphon the pain from my chest? Are you scared to feel it yourself? Maybe these thoughts just manifest the worst types of men, maybe I'm just not hiding my scars well enough.

### maneater

*in collaboration with spitfirebxxtch*
how do you tell her she's too loud when
you silenced her for centuries?

you tried to break her spirit
and relinquish all your demons.
it could have destroyed her,
but you didn't know
she was protected by
every woman
who ever felt the wrath of evil.

you cannot doubt a power
that has been
entrapped for so long;

you have twisted
her tongue, ripped out her teeth —
you didn't think she would stay silent,
did you?
she breathes vengeance
she bleeds retaliation
all that is in her is rebellion;
she is the revolution.

she is coming for you
she will get her revenge.

I'd let you **slice me open**,
slowly. I'll watch as you rub chunks
of salt into the wounds you created, as per
my request— I'll want you to look at me
while you do it.  look at me
while you do it, and I'll moan back in hymns
of sweet, sweet surrenderance

top it off with some honey infused
whiskey; pour it down my wrist
(*or wherever you would have chosen to rip me open,
just make it sting. honey is only needed
for the metaphor*)

this will be my ode to you, my submission.
I don't submit to anyone, but I'll
fall to my knees for you, if you wanted me to

I'd let you hurt me, baby
as long as I can feel something, anything—
I'd let you hurt me, baby
and I'll want you to look me in the eyes
as you pull the knife
from my soaked
caramelized
flesh.

## HEALED BUT NEVER FORGOTTEN

when your hand has
covered her mouth for so
long, when your hand has
gripped the flesh
and has bruised and broken
through, how do you expect
her not to flinch?
how do you expect her
not to cry?

no woman wants to relive
the past; how do you expect
her, not to be scared?
how do you expect her
not to question?
when your voice sounds so
much like her fathers
how can you expect her
to live life without fear
how can you expect her

to heal or to
to love easily
to forget her hurt
to forget the past –

you are foolish if you
think

her scars will heal with
time.
a pain like this,
an ache of this
magnitude
cannot be hushed away,
you are mistaken if you
think she'll
be quiet about this –
she wears her scars
proudly, not because
you made them but
because
she has survived –
and they will remain.

**to purge** to shed to let go of
to kill to finish to expunge to let rot
to get rid of to exercise out of to free myself from to lift the weight
to open the gates to see the horizon up ahead —

and to never
repent.

maneater

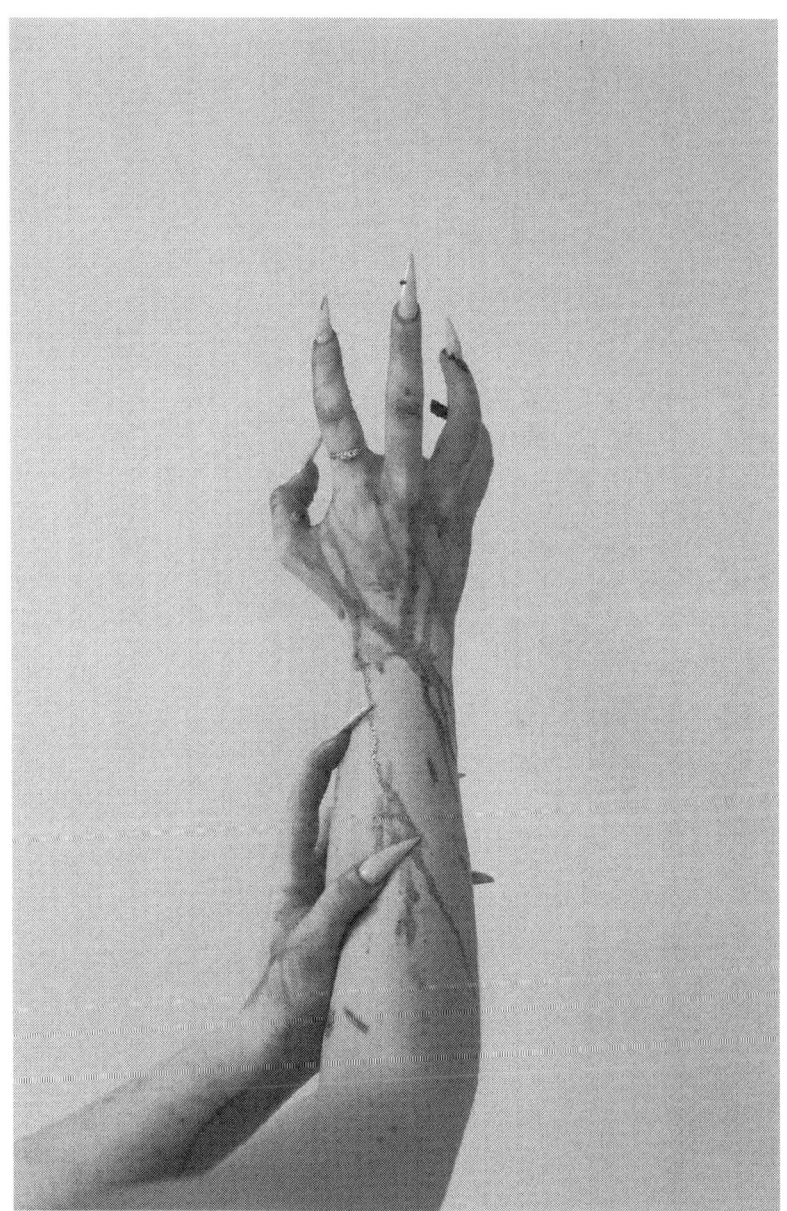

*Photo by T Gilliam*

My ex is a pedophile and is living his life like nothing is wrong. Like he didn't touch that 10 year old girl. Like he didn't touch me. Like he's forgotten what he's done. My ex is a pedophile and nobody knows what he does. What he did. But I do. And so does she. He's laughing at jokes on the internet and employed while girl and I struggle to make sense of this mess. When he delivers pizza to a house and a woman opens the door, will he violate her? Who will he rape when he's in a position of power? When he gets her alone? I have to wonder, will he still be laughing?

maneater

# confronting the monster

*you know who you are*

to dispel and kill the demon, you must name him first. to dispel and kill the demon, you must name him first. to dispel and kill the demon, you must name him first. to dispel and kill the demon, you must name him first. to dispel and kill the demon, you must name him first. to dispel and kill the demon, you must name him first. to dispel and kill the demon, you must name him first. to dispel and kill the demon, you must name him first. to dispel and kill the demon, you must name him first. to dispel and kill the demon, you must name him first. to dispel and kill the demon, you must name him first. to dispel and kill the demon, you must name him first.

maneater

**name them here** _____

jean-marie bub

**A MIRAGE OF WHAT I THOUGHT LOVE WAS,**
a ring in replacement of an apology
a trauma bond disguised as something more
a rape covered up with a title
a paper trail, exposing your pattern

we were both so young when you did things to us —
her, ten, completely unwilling,
ignorantly trusting in blood

me, fifteen
broken, easily persuaded,

you, sixteen when you forced her
to do things to you. she told me
what you made her do, you
stripped her of her innocence, you
made more than just a mistake, touching little girls
is not a mistake, you do understand it's
not a forgivable act, people like you aren't welcome to sit not
even with the murderers, even they can recognize that the blood
you shed and the trauma you gave gives little girls a different
kind of grave,

you, twenty-one when you came after me

## maneater

convincing no one but the child that i was with your
calculated backstory, your somber lies, you said you knew it
wasn't right, you
still picked me up late at night, you
told me love was a complicated thing. you said you knew it
was something i lacked, you
said you knew i'd always have to come back, you
said you respected me for never listening to my mother...

you made it out to be like you were in the category of
"other," monster,
you knew exactly what you were doing
you, predator

your friends told you i was bad news
not only because of my age, but
because it was me

and you heeded no warning.

you, a monster
her and i, ravished
not destroyed — we are stronger
than you
we are stronger
than this
i could use all the similes and metaphors

## jean-marie bub

to dance around just exactly what you are but i cannot afford
to hold this abhor closer to me anymore

and so when i'm finally forced
to hold the mirror to your face, when i peel back
the mask you've been hiding under for so long
don't be surprised, you would've had to have known that
your days in disguise would be numbered, you
spent four years of your life complimenting me on how i used
my voice, until i used it against you, you
will no longer masquerade as one of the good guys, you
will be thrusted into the light that you've always wanted to
avoid, you...

will not silence me as you did her, did you
really think i'd let more girls suffer at the hands of you?

your day to rot
is here.

maneater

fifteen

**YOU HEARD HIM WHEN HE TOLD YOU THAT HE LIKES TO "FIX" BROKEN GIRLS?** That he spends his nights fantasizing about the girls who are branded with daddy issues, scars, and burdens? Whether it's because "normal is boring," or "it's just better," the reason here doesn't matter. Were you paying attention when he let this secret leak out from his darkness, so sloppily, like it was nothing? Men like this have a vendetta. They spend their days wrist deep in boxes of cans, charring the back of their throats with leaf of their choice, and fixing up nice, perfectly straight white lines just to chase that feeling what we "broken girls" are running from — you heard him, right? So when the time comes, because, with men like this, it will - let him **think** that he saved you. Let him give himself all of the credit, even though when you broke, it was **you** that picked up the pieces while he watched. It was **you** who held him when **you** were falling apart and he had the audacity to make it about him. It was **you** who tried to make it work, it was you who was there for **YOU**... you see, they figure if they chase us, that maybe they'll finally get a chance to know what it feels like to break, too. That they'll get to be a part of the chaos, the late-night threats of suicide, the gradual breakdown of our minds — without having to feel it themselves. They feel invigorated at the sight of our demise, intoxicated when we tell them we need them. Let him believe that he fixed you — let him believe that he **saved** you. Let him believe that he is so god damn good at it so that when you abruptly chop the trauma bonds that grew wild like ivy in the space that exists between you and him, that you'll leave him wondering just how much of you was a mirage to begin with. Leave him stunned.

**Deer in headlights.**

Chop.

Chop.

*Chop.*

## jean-marie bub

**HE WILL COME TO YOU, IN NEED.** And you'll want to give. You'll want to hold him even though he's much larger than you. You'll want to carry his burdens for him. There will be something inside of you that'll ache to care for him, as if he was already yours. Something innate. But he'll be older than you. Maybe by 4 years, maybe by 6. But the difference will be there. And it will be noticeable. And your friends will make comments. And you will ignore them, because he will make you feel special, more special than anyone has before. And boy, do you swear you know more than everyone else. You'll doubt them. And he'll play it off by telling you that they're just jealous. You'll believe it because he'll speak to you differently. He'll tell you that you aren't like the other girls*he's been with before (*women. He'll call his past lovers "chicks" or "girls." He'll never use the word women). And you will feel validated because, at your young age, hearing that you're better than, or superior to, the older women that he's been with, will validate your young, insecure (and probably daddy-issue ridden) heart. But remember. This never was, and never will be, a competition. Didn't anybody tell you that men who prey on young women are losers? Didn't anyone ever tell you to be aware of the warning signs as they come? Didn't anyone ever – wait. They did. But you ignored them and listened to *him*. Him, being he who just met you. He who didn't even gain your trust yet. He who wore red flags like... red fucking flags. Red. Glaring. But listen... Its not your fault. Remember. This is why he chose you. Because you are young. Impressionable. Vulnerable. Remember when he said he wanted to fix a broken girl? Remember that stupid metaphor he used to make you feel better that one time he realized he insulted you when he called you damaged? The one about how "cracks let the light get in?" yeah. He probably saw that shit on fucking Instagram... but that's a piece of this fucked up puzzle. That's how he infiltrated your life. Your stability. Your peace. He is poison, and he got in. Remember when he said he wanted to fix a broken girl? Well. Here you are. There he is.

68

Except he's not fixing. He's breaking. Taking. Using. Bleeding you dry. He will make himself needed, although he will need you far more than you will EVER need him. You will shove him into all the voids you swore he'd fill. And for a moment, you will feel whole. Perhaps better than. Worthy, even. But it is an illusion. This was a mirage. This won't be your first encounter with abuse, but hopefully, once you realize (and you'll always realize when its far too late) it will be your last. Remember. He is a predator. You, the prey. There is only one thing you can do...

**RUN.**

## AN OPEN LETTER TO MY RAPIST
i wish i could instill MY pain within YOUR bones. i want darkness to feast on your carelessness — i want to watch as your sunny days suddenly transform into my cloudy nights. i want vengeance, in cold blood — i want to smell the fear radiating off your skin as if you were a doe caught in the mouth of a wolf — saliva dripping down your neck, i want you penetrated between the teeth of wrath. i want you defenseless. i want you on your back, paralyzed. baking under the vexation of the sun, watching as hundreds of people walk past your lifeless body while you barely muster enough energy from inside of your throat to call for help. i want you dragged through the mud. i want you tarred and feathered, i want every inch of your skin to itch at once as i tie your hands behind your back. i want to unleash an intrusion of cockroaches into the sleeves of your jacket and watch you squirm. i want you to feel it as i did. i want to ignore your cry's for help. i want to laugh in your face then turn the other way, as if i saw nothing at all — i want to suspend you. i want to put you at your desk by your lonesome and leave you with your thoughts, like child. i want them to become dark. i want you to think about how it would feel to jump. to cut. to swallow. to go. i want you to feel so desperate that you begin to naw at your flesh. i want you to pluck your eyelashes out of desperation, i want your skin to crawl upwards i want your hair to begin to break and fall out i want your chest to cave in and your brain to cave out i want you to feel it i want you to fucking feel as i felt when you left me there

## WE ONLY GO IN CIRCLES

bodies begging for more
than
this

am i deserving
of
this?

am i deserving
of
fingers shoved
down throat
knot in stomach?

thoughts taunt me in my sleep
what does leaving leave for me?
what does staying help me keep?

am i hoarding
these feelings

or shall i shed
my skin from doubt?
the doors revolve and i whisper
we only go in circles - that's all this ever was about.

## jean-marie bub

you can go to sleep while I pick the scabs off my face -
don't worry about me, I'll just be
busy
unearthing what's trying to heal

while you walk out on me,
and end this conversation on your own accord -

I'll spend my time spiraling
trying to figure out where I went wrong

- **GASLIT**

maneater

## AND I WONDER JUST HOW MUCH MORE I CAN TAKE –

how many more hours can i stand here

how many more bruises can coat my skin
(is there really any room left?)

scars flare and fall out
mind filled with doubt

how do i know when to leave
how to i know when it's too late

who do i turn to
am i all too late

who do i turn to,
am i all too late?

jean-marie bub

# FOR THE MOTHER'S THAT PROTECT THEIR RAPIST SONS
*for Nora*

You know what it's like to be young and vulnerable. To be pink and hairless and plump with innocence, to be all woman (in your head) and barely girl (when you were 15). You know all too well about the ocular paralysis of man and their drool that trails in blocks followed, the pursuit that forever changes the rhythm of your heart, the familiars that take things too far, the no's that went unheard, the hands that reached for you in darkness

I know you remember when skin scarred from being stretched too fast and the 32's that went to 36's, A's quickly to C's, when walking alone became an extreme sport...

Keys in hand and hand clutching purse, you've taught your daughter to cover curves and carry knife. You demand
that she come home when the sun is still up and you tell her not to wear her skirts too tight.

Estas pidiendo problemas, you tell her.
When faced with proof of the crime and daughters cries, you side with son. So I ask, is it because you're ashamed that this time it came from your own blood? Your sweat? Your tears? Are you afraid of looking at your son and seeing the eyes of your own rapist? Would accepting the truth mean accepting what happened to you?

maneater

if you ignore abuse you enable abuse
if you ignore abuse you enable abuse
if you ignore abuse you enable abuse
if you ignore abuse you enable abuse
if you ignore abuse you enable abuse
if you ignore abuse you enable abuse
if you ignore abuse you enable abuse
if you ignore abuse you enable abuse
if you ignore abuse you enable abuse
if you ignore abuse you enable abuse
if you ignore abuse you enable abuse
if you ignore abuse you enable abuse
if you ignore abuse you enable abuse
if you ignore abuse you enable abuse
if you ignore abuse you enable abuse
if you ignore abuse you enable abuse
if you ignore abuse you enable abuse
if you ignore abuse you enable abuse

jean-marie bub

*his family wanted proof
when all they had to do*

> Hi
>
> Im Dennis cousin, i saw your post and im in shock....

> Hi
>
> I know, I remember you from the family parties
>
> I would like to see poof of what you are saying
>
> There is a lot of history in my family of things that people just covers up or refuses to talk

*was look in mirror.*

# maneater

*Nobody earns abuse. It was never my fault.*

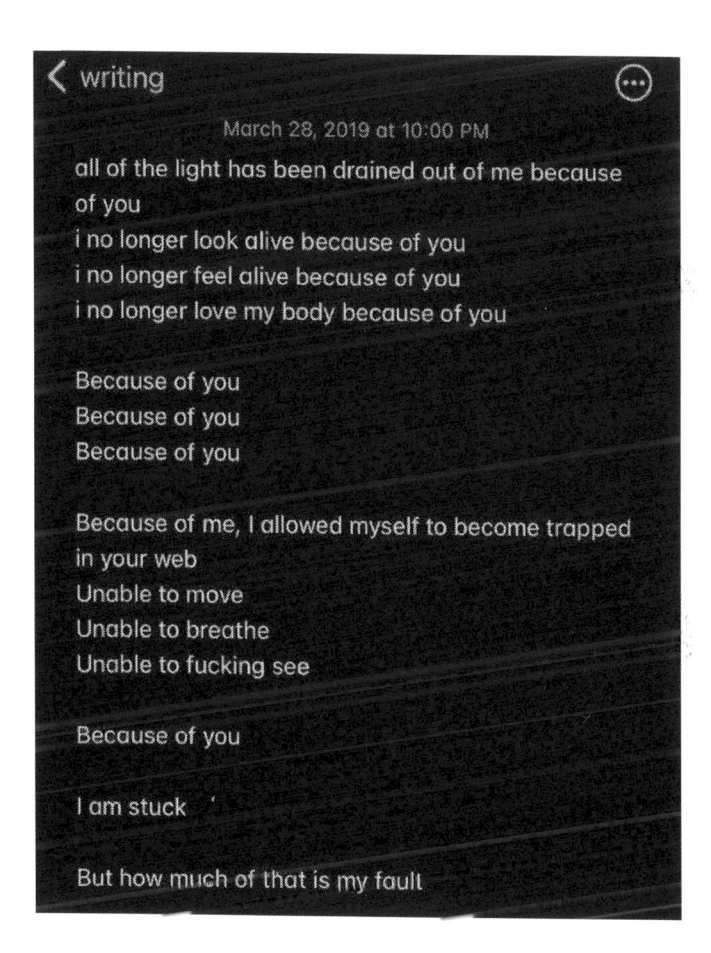

---

**‹ writing**

March 28, 2019 at 10:00 PM

all of the light has been drained out of me because of you
i no longer look alive because of you
i no longer feel alive because of you
i no longer love my body because of you

Because of you
Because of you
Because of you

Because of me, I allowed myself to become trapped in your web
Unable to move
Unable to breathe
Unable to fucking see

Because of you

I am stuck

But how much of that is my fault

jean-marie bub

**I know you miss my curves.**
I know you miss the regions of my body that
no one else has seen.
see,
you had docked your boat on my private island,
my unexplored territory...
after seeing all of the bountiful resources I had possessed,
after drinking from my fountain
of impermeability.
you tended to my gardens and took care of the flowers
you made sure to keep everything just as you liked it
but one day you decided to plant trees
that were far too foreign for my soil.
hesitantly, I accepted this.
consequently
you cut them down.

I was perfect for your relentless manipulation,
for I was untouched
you had decided that I was yours.
you set fire to my foliage
you ravaged through my garden, uprooting my flowers
killing most vibrant life.

And even after being kicked out the garden of Eden –

I know you still miss my curves
you can probably still feel the indentation of my waist
you probably still have a very vivid picture of what my island
used to look like,
before you attempted force me into submission.

I do remember your hands
and how they felt amongst the petals

### maneater

and the leaves -

I know you miss my curves
but no part of me
will ever come close to missing your
poison;
never will I submit to a man
who tries to pin me down underneath his grip -

I rather burn slowly
and have all life devastated
than ever letting you graze my terrain,

      again.

## THIS IS MY HEX FOR YOU
You will be stuck in that town until your dying days.
Every plant you buy will quickly rot and decay
Your back will never feel a moment with no pain,
Your bud won't get you high no more, every spliff you roll will canoe, Raws will always come packaged with no glue
You'll wonder why everything you touch seems to die
Every fruit you buy only after a day will mold and spoil,
Every woman you glance at will cringe at your face, and
You'll always inevitably be replaced.
Bills larger than ten will land in the shredder
Every morning when you wake up, things still won't get better, no matter how hard you pray, it'll fall upon deaf ears
You'll develop 57 different kinds of irrational fears
Abscess upon abscess will crowd your skin
From your left eye will leak blood, red — projecting your sins
Not even the church will have a use for you,
You'll find no purpose, not even at the bottom of Don Julio 1942
Parents will have to stop when they see your face, just to point and tell their children never to become such a disgrace
You'll never be able to make more than minimum wage
Sevenfold, you'll never not be in discomfort and pain
For every woman you've ever hurt, there'll be another hell for you to visit, you'll be reincarnated as a bastard rat,
no caste system could ever free you from a suffering like that
You'll be a victim of the fate that Poseidon should've faced, that's the punishment for rape, not even all your crimes
I want you to remember that Medusa isn't the one who get snakes in this story, instead of turning women to stone, it'll be your face, frozen down to bone.
This isn't an allegory, I mean this all literally
sword to cut and rope to bind, these words will find you in every lifetime.

### maneater

And when the earth finally spits you out I hope it leaves you fucking raw, intestines wrapped around neck, like a cat that's been declawed

                That's what you get for doing me dirty —
      you're not even a man and you're damn near thirty.

jean-marie bub

𝔐edusa isn't the one who get snakes in this story
𝔐edusa isn't the one who get snakes in this story
𝔐edusa isn't the one who get snakes in this story
𝔐edusa isn't the one who get snakes in this story
𝔐edusa isn't the one who get snakes in this story
𝔐edusa isn't the one who get snakes in this story
𝔐edusa isn't the one who get snakes in this story
𝔐edusa isn't the one who get snakes in this story
𝔐edusa isn't the one who get snakes in this story
𝔐edusa isn't the one who get snakes in this story
𝔐edusa isn't the one who get snakes in this story
𝔐edusa isn't the one who get snakes in this story

## maneater

I remember that time you drove me out to some big parking lot behind two corporate offices off the highway, which was our usual spot, because, you know, I was 15 and you were 21 and you had to hide us for the first six months - and when we had finally settled in the backseat of your dads car, I showed you a poem I had written for English class.

> *"this is great but, how much more can you possibly write about pain?"* he asked.

And after damn near six years, I finally found the answer to your question.
### FOR AS LONG AS MEN LIKE YOU EXIST.

You've made it so that I'm forced to grow eyes for skin, doubting my own thoughts, putting my keys in fist when a man does so much as smile in my direction. I steer clear from skateparks in fear I'll find you there. Every three weeks I pay to have my nails crafted into weapon. I can't wear headphones walking alone, I have to tell my lovers to please not wear your cologne - you have turned me into lie detector, hawk and mouse, shrinking myself into child when need be and channeling the screams I should've used in your room when confronted on the street with another you.

I had to plan my escape from you, and so now, every exit is premeditated.

### jean-marie bub

i'm able to talk again today.
throat clear of sin.

yesterday, i stumbled over words.

for years
this tongue has been

soaked in regret,
teeth          rotting.

maneater

collapse the systems that make it hard
for survivors to speak out about abuse
collapse the systems that make it hard
for survivors to speak out about abuse
collapse the systems that make it hard
for survivors to speak out about abuse

### jean-marie bub

*use the space to vent below*

maneater

# loud noises & men's voices

*"love breaks my bones and I laugh"*
Charles Bukowski

jean-marie bub

the difference is simple —
your scars are metaphor.

mine maim the entirety of my skin
and everything else i hide within.

## maneater

Have you ever held the blade to your wrist? Have you ever dripped from your bedroom to the sink? Do you remember how you reacted the first time you hit the third layer of skin? Do you remember the look on your moms face when you told her what you did? Do you remember the veins? The pencil sharpener? The shrapnel? The pain? Or no pain at all? Can you still feel the itch under your skin? Upwards, like Satan trying to inch his way back up to God? For vengeance. What do you think he'd want to tell him? What were you trying to say when you made all those gashes on your flesh? What do you have to say about them now?

## jean-marie bub

sometimes I think that living is disgusting
we take everything out just to put it all away

you become so depressed you can only live outward, spilling
pouring your hatred,
everywhere
trying to collect yourself on city streets

contemplating the blade
before walking into work.

maneater

I make the decision to hurt myself hours before actually doing so. It is not an impulsive act. It is a premeditated one.

Step one. I get **the itch**.

Step two. Itch does not cease to exist.

Step three. I decide, then and there, whether I'm at a park, at dinner with a friend, handing a customer their change, or opening my eyes for the first time in the day — it'll happen today. Hours from now.

Step four. Crave.

Step five. I'm walking to my car. Saying bye to my friend. Clocking out of work. Getting out of bed — I decide, which vice. Lighter, blade, fist.

Step six. Blade always wins. I'm probably painting now. Writing, maybe, but not likely. Writing is a reflective act. Premeditative too. So I'm painting. Or in the shower. Something. The itch resurrects itself in what feels like cicadas in tree in summer. A pulsating, unignorable nuisance. The urge becomes stronger, but I must wait. Impulsiveness only makes a mess. With every stroke, I remember where all my necessary tools are located in my room. I paint the stem of a flower. Extra-large Band-Aids. Second to last bottom drawer. I begin outlining the leaves. Paper towels, to my left. I must remember to not use all of them while painting; I'll need several sheets for the mess. I open a tube of red paint. It oozes out into the canvas. I paint the petals. Rubbing alcohol. Behind the vintage DIY books my father passed down to me. To sterilize the wound. This is a premeditated act. I begin shading in the flower. White, yellow and orange coats my brush. Colors bleed into the crimson. The blade. Buried in a reusable tote bag stuffed somewhere in my dresser. I add depth to the painting. Salt, on my bed stand. To cleanse my space, but also, to feel it deeply. My phone. Next to me. In case I get carried away. I sign my name in the bottom right corner.

Step seven. Hours have passed. I've probably said hello to you, had a conversation with you, and as you said bye, you'd have seen me smile as we parted. "How much better she's gotten," you'd tell your mother as we head towards opposite horizons. How unknowingly wrong you'd be. I go out for pizza and watch as the counter girl slices through the dough and cheese. Sauce oozes out. The itch is back. I haven't forgotten about it. "Stay strong," she says, but I'd have made up my mind hours ago. She must've seen the scars on my wrist. This is not an impulsive act.

Step eight. I get home and I open the door. I step in quietly. I can hear the cicadas echo inside of me. In the back of my head, I can hear my boyfriend telling me to put music on. Music is only a distraction. I must focus.

## maneater

Step nine. I shower. This is a ritual. The skin must be clean, completely. I must have asked the moon to cleanse me of the energy that weighs heavy on my soul. I tell it, this sacrifice will be for you. In return, please — get this shit out of my head. Water rushes over me. I feel magnetic. I pace myself. I breathe in deeply. This is a premeditative act.

Step ten. I'm naked in bed. I size myself up. Thigh. Wrist. Stomach. Ankle.

Step eleven. Rubbing alcohol.

Step twelve. Blade in hand.

Step thirteen. I know you would rather me end this with me putting down the blade, but this is a poem. If you were paying attention before, I told you, for me, poems are a premeditated act. A reflective one. The truth. This isn't going to end as you hoped.

Step fourteen. Itch turns fire as I take blade to skin.

Step fifteen. Paper towels. 8 sheets. The heavy-duty kind. Bandaid(s). I put music on.

Step sixteen. This is a ritual.

breathe in breathe out
breathe in breathe out
breathe in breathe out
breathe in breathe out
breathe in breathe out
breathe in breathe out
breathe in breathe out
breathe in breathe out
breathe in breathe out
breathe in breathe out
breathe in breathe out
breathe in breathe out
breathe in breathe out
breathe in breathe out
breathe in breathe out
breathe in breathe out
breathe in breathe out
breathe in breathe out
breathe in breathe out
breathe in breathe out

maneater

 

I only realize how much damage has been done when the night fades into morning. Cut marinates into bruise and aches at the surface — sun glares down, judgingly. The corners of my lips no longer lift at the sight of destruction.

In her face, I see the shame. She knows what I've done. She rises, and she knows all too well, autumn has come again. I am changing. I am trying - the rising sun as my witness.

jean-marie bub

my pain,
this wreckage
this immense intensity of
invigorating insanity

has plummeted me to
the very
bottom.

the bottom
of the glass
the rock
the cliff
the sea —

all that's left
is to go through the motions
and to endure
the duration of the mind.

maneater

There is a man screaming belligerently on the train. Everyone switches cars at the next stop. I stay seated and close my eyes. It feels like home.

## jean-marie bub

Lyn said that I'm my ancestor's wildest dreams but
I have a feeling I'm their worst fucking nightmare

I pull skin back in attempts to verify that I exist
Plucking on vein like guitar string, I
Tune my body to adjust to the pain
And hum to the melody that trauma plays

Day by day I chip away at what they gave me
Wishing to rip the meat off these hips, praying to
Suck the fat out my cheeks, bone dry, I
Cry until there's no water in my blood left, I

Make altar to honor them and to apologize for my sins
And then I starve them of their foods and potions.
Mold forms in water and mosquitos breed, I place paint and receipts on top of the fallen leaves

I'm supposed to be paying homage to their timeline, but I'm seemingly stuck going through phrases where I deny that these powers are mine.

And even after the neglect they still beg to be fed
*come back to us*
They whisper in my dreams – their hands reach out,
pulling at my bed.

maneater

jean-marie bub

moans that sing in hymns of honey
are halted by what feels like knives

cervical pain pulsates through my veins
and suddenly, i realize
the sun beaming through the blinds
can't save me.

## maneater

**COLONIZER** mixed with slave, i shouldn't be who i am, you see, i am refugee and invader, puta y gringo — how unsettling is it to know that i've murdered the other half of me, that i've created profit off the flesh of my ancestors, that i've slain and have been slain. how unsettling is it to know that half of me has rioted, revolted, revolutionized entire cities in hopes for liberation while the other half of me has caged me, raped me, murdered me, oppressed me for centuries. perhaps my roots are so terrified of one another, that they have plagued me with these imbalances, these mistakes, these illnesses to divide themselves as they have in each uprising, each chance at freedom, each chance at damnation. i am war. i am famine. i am every exposed rib pressing against my ancestors stomach, i am every glutton laughing at the deprivation.

i am the island of Hispaniola. i have arrived alongside Columbus, but it is my hand on the chopping block. blood pours off the shore and bleeds into the sea filling the Caribbean with the corruption of the colonizer, filling it with the truth. it begins to seep out of the islands of my sisters — the Beginning is coming.

i am revolution trapped within a confederate nightmare. the blood has been spilt on both sides and has mixed to form a proper monster and, it's me

- mestiza / identity crisis

**mind confined** with lying lines of I'm fine
too sick to move
sick enough to find time to rhyme
these feelings inside
are based off all kinds of lies

I'm fine,
I'm fine.

maneater

AND
I
KNOW
THERE'S
NO
PLACE
LIKE
HOME
BECAUSE
I
HAVENT
FOUND
IT
YET

jean-marie bub

everywhere I go
my back is to wall. I map out exits and entrances.
the only thing you were good at teaching me
was how to plan my next escape.

maneater

i wanted
you to
unearth me.
i wanted you
to pick the weeds
from my garden, to
reap the rewards of my
harvest, to keep coming back
for when i bloomed, but instead,

you wrecked me.

you took my petals and discarded them
as if i hadn't just grown towards
what i thought was the sun —
as if i hadn't just grown
my roots into
the palm of
your hand

jean-marie bub

Being alone with my **brokenness** is perhaps the most dangerous thing.

maneater

*after the great Nia Mora*

Atticus, Bukowski and R.H. Sin rhyme us petty lines to profit off our pain, forever contorting repeated words, regurgitating garbage into mouths that were conditioned by society to remain open for it to pour in.

Man tries to sell you a cure for pain, when man is exactly what you're trying to heal yourself from.

Throw it the fuck out and listen to your sisters. Do not buy these books. Do not buy into the lie that men know how to quantify heartbreak. Read Nia Mora. Read Lyn Patterson. Read Shanice Ariel. Read Jessica Paige Ballen. Natalia Vela. Nadera. Read the greats. And read them well.

We must always return to our sisters
in order to heal ourselves.

remember to hold vigil for all the versions of yourself you've had to sacrifice & kill to become this current version of you. make sure to visit their wandering bodies in the hallways you left them in. hold their hand & forgive them. remember to honor the softness of the skin you had shed previous to this one. thank vessel for their lesson. caress the face of fourteen-year-old you and tell them that somewhere far, far away from the town they remain stuck in, you have lit a candle for them. tell them that you wail for them if you do. tell them how they'd love to see how the sunset looks in your new 2 bedroom in the city. that every time it sets, you're reminded of them. give them the letters you've shoved under your bed.

because thirty years from now you will remember this version of yourself to be as young and as naïve as fourteen-year-old you – and just as you've had to kill the ones in the past, you'll have to kill this current version of you, the one whose reading reading this, too.

maneater

b roken since i did what i did
r egret soaks my skin and
i can't move on from you, my
s oulmate, my love
e veryday i think about my sins.
i can't begin to explain, the
s un left earth the day i pushed you away, but

what was done had to be done.
in another life, i stayed.

jean-marie bub

/i've never stepped foot in an airport but jesus fucking christ
do i know what it's like to leave everything behind/

## maneater

if i try hard enough i can remember far back. back to when things were normal back to when you danced with me in the rain, unafraid, unconcerned with the dark matter that'd eventually take over your mind. if i try hard enough i can repress the anger that you inflicted upon me, causing me to hate and tear myself apart. i can replace the alcohol in your hand with coffee instead, i can pretend that it was all normal. if i try hard enough i can dismiss the many memories i have without you there, and i can try to replace them with the cloudy remnants i've compiled and stored in a small bookshelf in the corner of my brain that contain moments of your genuine and childish grin. i can see you standing in my doorway, drink not yet opened, light gleaming onto your face, hand resting softly on the wall, and for once your knuckles looked soft, lively, and unscathed. for once i can remember a moment of peace and serenity within your being, for once i can remember looking relief in the face. suddenly i'm daydreaming about how differently the cards could've been dealt — i find myself thinking of the father you could've been, but never turned out to be.

### jean-marie bub

you chose the alcohol
because you knew
it was the only thing
that wouldn't leave you.

## maneater

you are so soft. even when you came home at night from working all day, you were always so soft. everything about you. your hands, veiny. I remember examining them, palm up, and open. you let me touch your hands. soft. like your hair, which you would always swat me away from. soft. like silk. in the summer, the sun touches you and makes you blonde. magic, silk gold. you comb your soft fingers through your soft, silky hair. in the summer you smile and your garden blooms. you move the soil around with your soft hands and out come soft flowers. your cheeks, even when you had stubbles from the beard you never finished growing, soft. your voice, when you call the grocery clerks "sweetheart," or when you tell me a story, soft. your hugs are soft. even though we dont hug all the way or for too long, the clothes you wear are always so soft. the zip up jackets you wear, cozy, cigarette ridden, but somehow that makes you warm. the way your eyes light up when you hear me say "i love you," and you know it's no longer forced — soft. you are soft, on the outside...

but I know the cold, stern parts of you. believe me. I've seen the scary, the spitting, the yelling. I've stared at the empty seat next to mom at graduations, picturing you there. searching for you in the crowd, I always thought I'd find you. I'd craft you into a mirage, hoping you'd appear. I've felt the void of you, for all the years that you were absent, yet just a set of stairs below my bedroom. could you hear me crying? did you ignore it, or could you just not hear my pleads to just be held over the blasting sound of your tv? I remember how your eyes filled with rage, fists clenched the first time I told you I hated you. I still feel the ache from your knuckles, I can still feel the sting in my chest from the words that spilled out from your poison filled belly — but I choose to remember you soft. silk gold, soft.

jean-marie bub

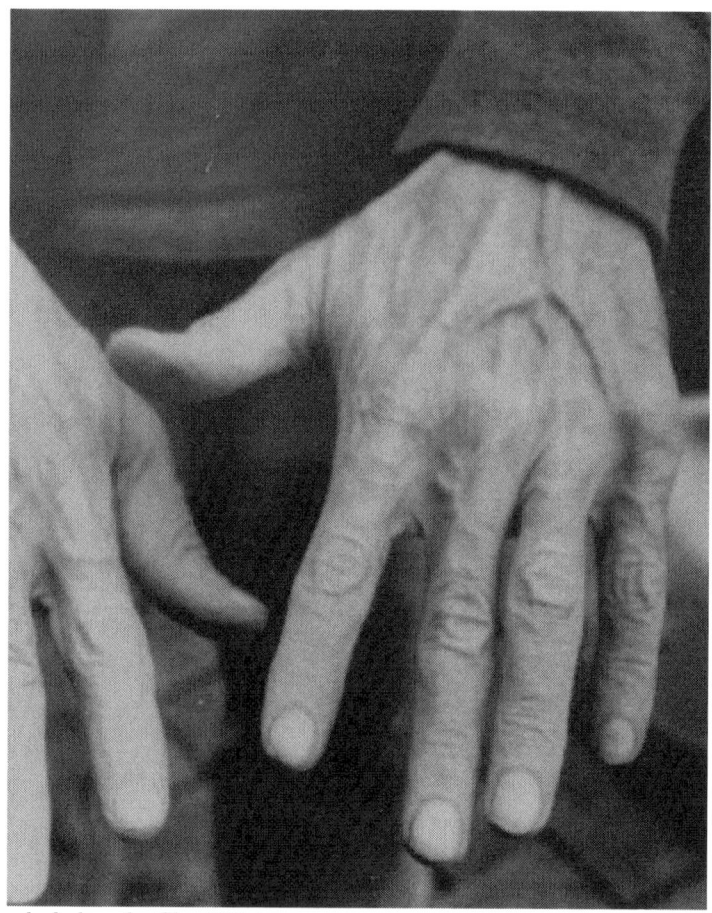

*dads hands, film 2014*

maneater

I want to be alone in my emptiness. Painfully numb, heart with all its **vacancies and knives** in hand, in all their stainless-steel glory. I want to be surrounded by nothingness. No couch, no bed, no canvas, no lamp. Only a window. a single window that spans from floor to ceiling — a window that illuminates the room so that I'm able to tell where my wrist begins and ends. For the knife. I need the light for the knife. And to remind myself just how lonely it can all get— if I decide to throw away the keys.

jean-marie bub

# for the men i've eaten...

maneater

NOV 1, 4:17 AM

Yo

I guess the full moon got me thinking bout you lol

### jean-marie bub

when i write about men,
do i trap them here in these pages?

                                         is doing so a spell or a curse?

every man i write about becomes trapped
between these lines.

maneater

loyalty
loyalty
loyalty

&
&
&

liars
liars
liars

don't
don't
don't

mix
mix
mix

jean-marie bub

## EYE-FUCK

I want you
to fill my valley
with your streams, I
want you to make me plentiful,

I want you to plant seeds that
root chrysanthemums inside of me,
I want you to
sow my soil and
reap the rewards of
its fertility,

I want you to pour yourself into a glass
so that I can sip from you slowly
while I watch the sun rise in some
distant land that reminds me of you,
I want to feel every inch of you.
slide down my throat and
into my stomach, I want to enjoy
every last drop of your holiness —

I want you to make me plentiful
and I
would like you          to watch.

###### maneater

i can see us
somewhere in the future of
this planet –

we are running,
we are laughing,
we are drinking.

we are drunks,
the soil and
the both of us.

we can never quite
get enough.

we are yearning to quench our everlasting vigor,
a form of thirst that only we can only fortify via each other.

we are reaching up to the sun in only prayer.

we extend our extremities in hopes for an answer,
just as the vines that reside next to us seem to do out of instinct.
we are basking in vulnerability,
perfectly permeable to the toxins,
yet we are still drinking,
us and the soil.

the soil shows no mercy.
the roots that lie within seem to
retain every single last drop
of the viable potion

but here we are,

### jean-marie bub

fearful of the drink that pours
before us,
the same drink that
the plants sip so eloquently upon,
fearful of the bountiful droplets
that moistens our skin
and make love to the dirt...
we are running.

we are running in attempt to escape
the tingling sensation within our bones,
we flee like intoxicated urchins,
like mad men,
like two lovers under the rain.

the sun takes cover behind the clouds
and urges us to save ourselves.

we are still running.

we are drunk off the rain,
the soil
and
the both of us.

maneater

/silk sheet lover
dripping in gold –

the moon dresses me in desire
and you strip it off of me with your tongue/

### jean-marie bub

sad music pours out of my speakers as I undress
your eyes on my chest,
notes of black cherry and lavender bleed out of the walls,
the room swells with a deep
sweet, I want you

on your knees
                                   begging
                salivating,
**Pavlov's dog...**

                    english ivy cascades down bookshelves as
                       orange hues echo throughout the room
                pink salt illuminates my curves on your thighs
                            my want blooms into

            an irresistible lust.
              I ring my bell.

## maneater

i have given you my all
expecting nothing in return,
for the men in my past
have taken everything and left
me with nothing.

you, my love
you emptied your soul into mine
fulfilling my dreams and
forming my broken heart
whole —
you, my love
are liberation unlike no other

you.
are justice
for all the times they've robbed me
of my
sanity
sexuality
sacrifice
solitude
spirituality —
you.
are justice
in its purest form
you are as dangerous as revenge.

jean-marie bub

loving him is cathartic.

that's the problem.

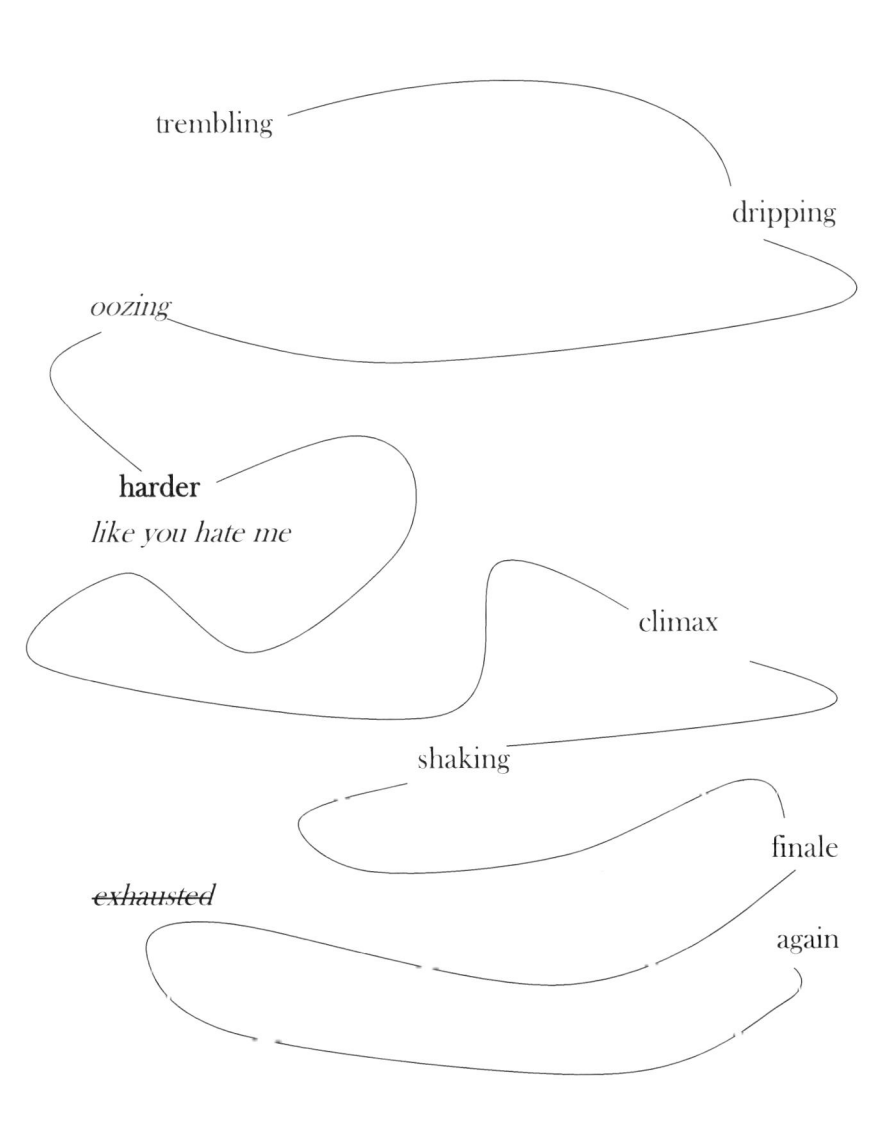

maneater

trembling

dripping

*oozing*

**harder**
*like you hate me*

climax

shaking

finale

~~exhausted~~

again

**THESE HANDS MEND**
these hands would worship you
hold you
love you tender
if you'd let them
but you won't let them
so they'll sit still,
and they'll remain unmoved
until you make yours

maneater

# Lesson #222

# Do not rush to healing without first completely feeling all seasons of pain.

*let the anger simmer.*

#### jean-marie bub

every notification becomes a trigger. every

      bloop

            bing

                   ding

is followed by nails penetrating skin, a buffer
between confrontation       and delusion

hair falls out as
skin dries

mom asks if you're okay, and
you just won't be able to explain.

                                          pain.

### maneater

gifts only came when the blood ran thick.
oozing down my arm,
coagulated for weeks but
you only notice now, even though
you watched the blood dry
some even got on your hands but
you wiped it on your pants and
chalked it up to an inconvenience

so you get me flowers
you pluck each petal
and before they can scream
**"HE LOVES YOU YOU NOT"**
you stick them onto my bloodied flesh,
assuming they can heal my wounds, but
your gift just infects my cut

i ignore the gunshots that flare red.
i know exactly how it'll end — and i'll love to watch it crash and burn

### jean-marie bub

what an unfortunate truth that trickled out of the corner of that pretty mouth / heart no longer encased in sin / or whatever form of karma your god seems to believe in / i wanted to love you but you spit me out before you even tasted me / this is a betrayal / I will never be able to accept / love / cannot / save me

### maneater

gums swollen with goodbye and you, at my feet
tearing at my Achilles

with teeth bleeding and tongue limp with ache,
i plead with you for the last time –

i have given you tendon and blood and bone.
even with this earth warming into puddles, you still come
to destroy the last salvageable parts of me

even Venus cries out, begging of you to let me go.

## DEATH IN THE AFTERNOON
tar drenched lung drips in sync with
liver filled with liquor; i carve a hole to cut it out
wringing from my organ the poison you left behind,
i wish nothing more than to break this bind, but heart
can't help but ache

>    at
>    thought of you
>    gone

i used to pour cognac to match the hurt of the blade you left
in my back, but as time pass i realize
i need something stronger than that

moon water over malachite i channel every ancestor.
i beg them to talk sense into this

>    tired body, melancholy
>    bones break

last resort, i don't trust fate to ensure we separate.
two tapers tied with twine on my alter begin to burn

>    i will mourn the death
>    of our love in every lifetime

I gather the ashes of our rope and place them in urn.

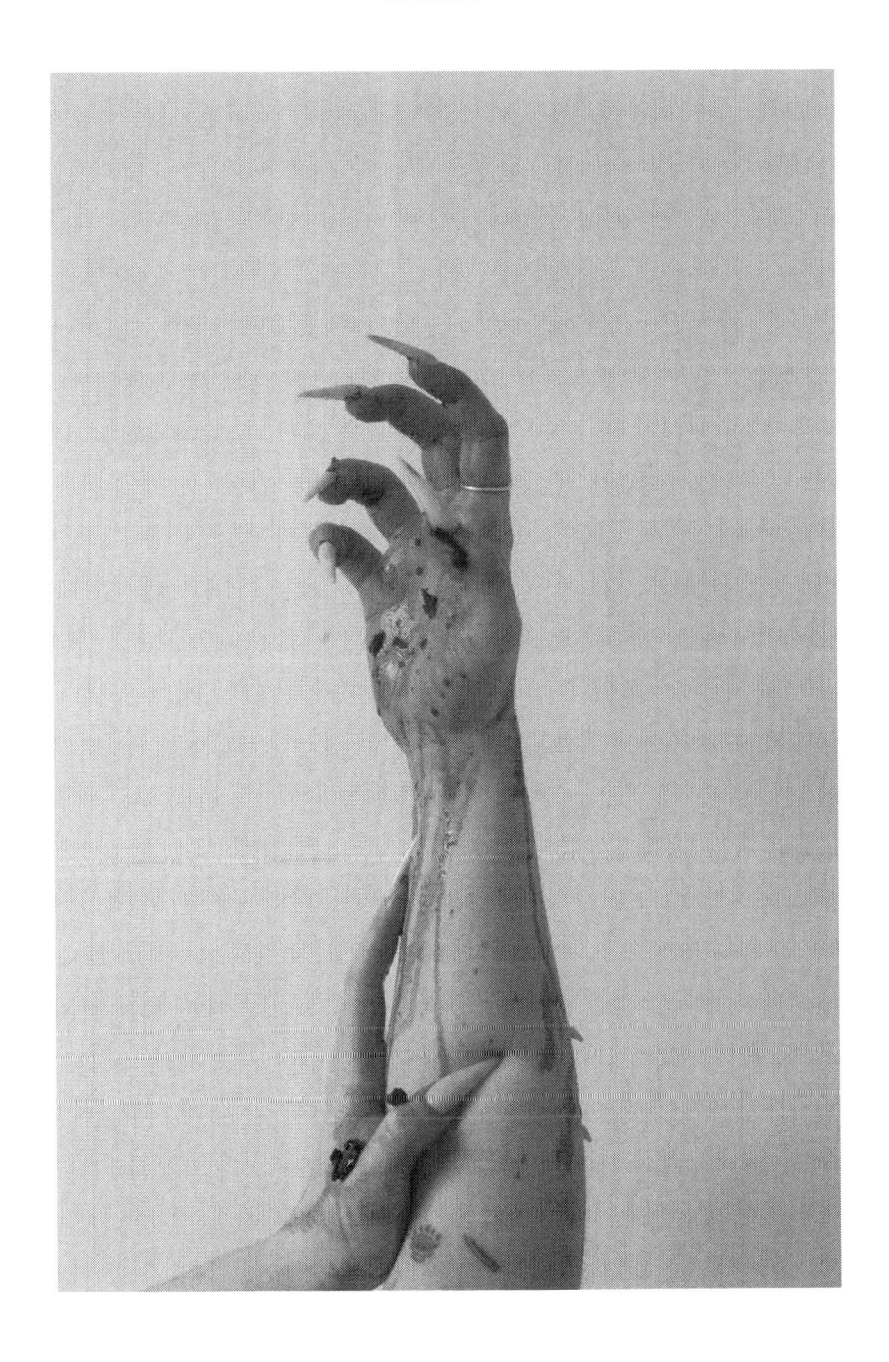

maneater

jean-marie bub

## PURGE. CLEANSE. REPEAT.

purge yourself of all that hurts
you can't just slap cotton over wound –
you must expel the demon
in its entirety. rip him
out of you. violently. it's the only way

any small glimpse of kindness,
and he'll stay.

this act will hurt
but you know its what's best
remember --

                                there's much more solitude
                                        in loneliness.

### maneater

I will no longer stop you from throwing yourself at women who could care less about the pain that was caused in youth that you can't forget. The ache you can't get rid of. The one you itch to talk about without having to explain. I won't stop you from subconsciously pouring your heart out (because you know that's what it is) to pretty women who will abandon you after seeing your eyes flare red, to strangers who won't know what to do with the holes of your heart, to bodies that will only listen to your voice to fill the void of their own silence. My throat is raw from explaining. My hands cut from holding the mirror to your face.

So I'll let you learn through lesson. I'll leave, or maybe you'll leave first. But this time, for you, will be different. Everything's been so easy to replace for you, but even the color of her nail polish will remind you of me. You'll be driven mad searching for the scent of me in the pillows of people in your call list. And even the new ones you find online or in bars will size you up and spit you out after a taste, maybe two due to your charm. But they'll know. They'll taste the longing on your tongue. One woman after another or many at once, your eyes have always been too big for your stomach. I've come to accept (after months of trying to convince myself otherwise) that I'll have to leave you lonely. And you'll convince yourself that you're okay. That will only last until you realize you cannot conquer what always leaves.

Years after me will, in time, turn into years of you trying to find someone that will hold you like I did. That will know every inch of you like I did. That will stitch your wounds like I did. That will fuck you like I did...

And after all I have given you, you will be standing alone in the space you didn't know how to make your own, empty. Clutching onto the past, revisiting the Polaroids I left for you that'll be wrinkled and stained — still, after all these years, wandering aimlessly, trying desperately to fill your voids.

this love could last a lifetime,
but not with someone like you.

I loved you so.
But I'm forced to let go.

maneater

## Lesson #333

### Once you realize that men cheat to conquer instead of to hurt, you'll feel a lot better about your position in all of this.

*They are weak. All they can conquer is pink matter, and the only form of validation they can get is from the sexual acceptance of another body. That's their own problem to solve. This is a sign for you to let go and evolve.*

### jean-marie bub

#### *in collaboration with Jessica Paige Ballen*

This isn't a suicide note, though I'm sure you'd expect that from a crazy bitch like me. This is a love letter with blade sealing envelope. I hope this finds you well (done), cooked from the inside out. charred and unrecognizable, understand these words as they come out;

I cut the brakes from your car. Filled your shower with a thousand bees and held the door. Grabbed you by the Adam's apple that you didn't have to pay for like sister Eve; you broke my back so I've decided I'll break your fucking neck. Did you really think I didn't have any cards left in my deck?

Your first mistake was underestimating the beast. I eat men like you, the ones who see woman and think feast, I *devour* men like you

With my forehead cradled in the crook of your neck, I plot your death as you slept. Fantasied of liver dangling at tongue, of carving my name into your abdomen, of prying wound open with nail and massaging your intestines before dinner. I've dreamt of killing you over and over, the same way you killed me. As you breathed in, I imagined your last breath out. I assure you, this is love. The gaslight isn't so thick now, is it? Can't you see clearly through the mists? Poor baby. Breaking me was the only thing you were good at. Breaking me in and breaking me down, but this ends once I stop coming around. The purpose you served was to relinquish powers buried in centuries of shame, decades of women scorned by man, by your stupid little games. By ending this cycle with you, I end their suffering too.

    and this is exactly why     i devour men like you.

maneater

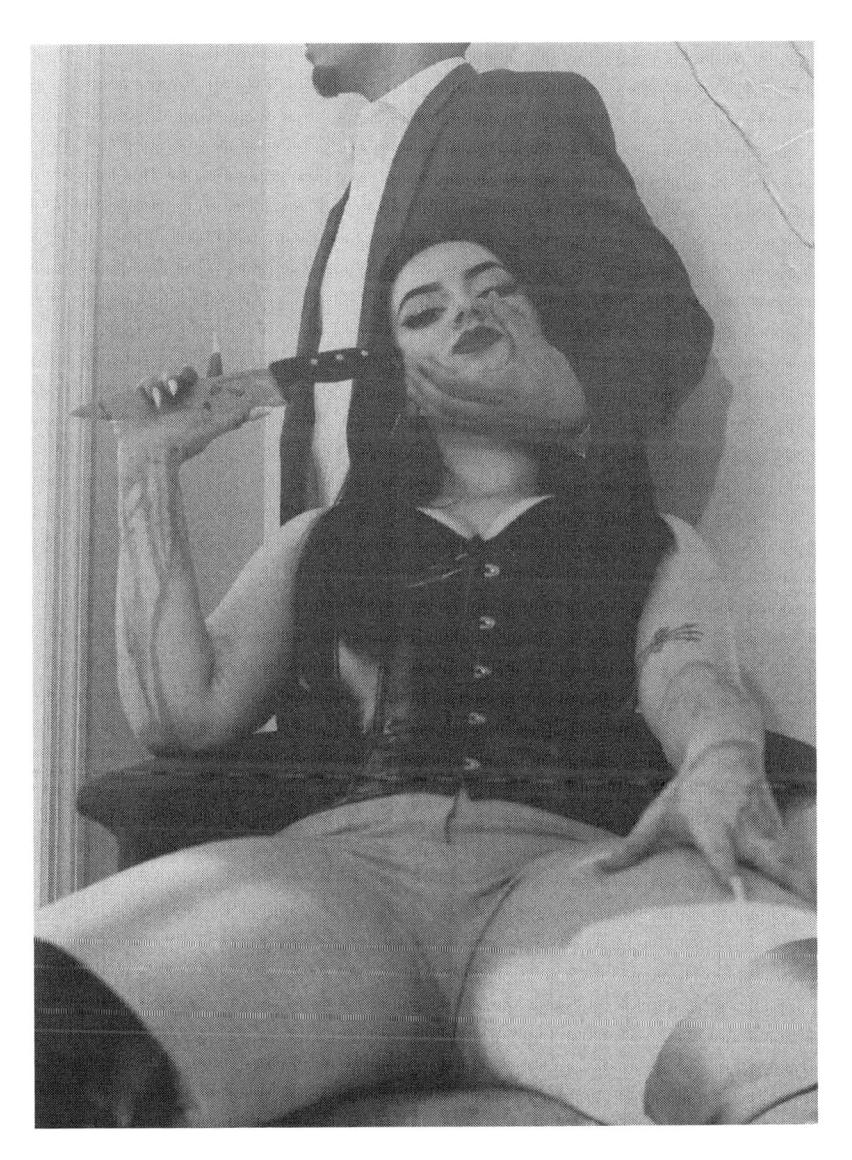

*Photo by T Gilliam*

jean-marie bub

*in collaboration with Nadera*

I had sworn you'd taken pieces of me with you when you left that night. sun to moon, it took me thousands of rotations to realize -   body is not a thing to be coveted

**body heals me body loves me body houses this soul.**

**IT IS ME WHO HOLDS THE POWER
IT IS ME WHO HOLDS THE POWER
IT IS ME WHO HOLDS THE POWER**

**I am body I am being I am whole.
what is mine has always been, you could never taint this soul.**

thousands of rotations later, I affirm —
I could never relinquish my power.

these hands, mine
always knowing where to go,
what to do
goosebumps trailing where they've been,
where they're going
skilled, fervent, determined
roaming free, against

this flesh, mine
overflowing
glistening with sweat
warm to taste, soft to bite
eager tastebuds gliding with ease
between the rise and fall of breasts, where
these nipples, mine

## maneater

sensitive, taut, hard

this back, mine
off from sheets already damp
arched with ass positioned for what's to come
legs spread, trembling
fingers searching, finding
this apex, mine
these lips, mine
this clitoris, mine
these folds, mine
throbbing, pulsating
willingly opening up

to this entrance, all fucking mine
and gushing with power

what is mine and has always been mine alone.

it is me who holds the power
it is me who holds the power
it is me who holds the power
it is me who holds the power
it is me who holds the power
say it louder
it is me who holds the power
it is me who holds the power
it is me who holds the power
it is me who holds the power
it is me who holds the power
say it louder
it is me who holds the power
it is me who holds the power
it is me who holds the power
it is me who holds the power
it is me who holds the power

## AFFIRMATION FROM THE BODY

harborer of humanity
(if you choose)
harborer of you

i am yours,
but i am not you

i am vessel of the soul
omnipotent omnipresent omniparent
connector to the physical world

i am portal i am magical i am flesh
i am blessed to have been picked as vehicle for you
enamored in love forever indebted
to you

### final girl

i am the weapon that will prosper against
you. the gun will not falter. the knife will
always splice through skin, smooth

i eat men like plath. i rip flesh
with my teeth, slowly sucking
skin off bone, bone out of skin.
i eat men like you.

you stand before me, shocked, as if you
expected every woman to cower in your
presence, to remain silent like the hostages
you've held here before.

i break cycle with each syllable that falls from
my open mouth. i wasn't the first girl you
hurt, but i vow to be the final one.

truth slips off tongue, and with terror, you
realize –
not only have i survived you, but i'm coming
back for what's mine.

maneater

*Photo by T Gilliam*

## RED BRUSHSTROKES
*By Joaquin T. Capeheart*

She is a woman
born in fire
forged In the inferno
fierce in presence
eye all seeing
She is piercingly insightful
depths of her soul scoured
pounded by pressure.
Light still present in abundance
exhausting mining but divine timing
resulted in her excavated diamonds
She is fueled by
meals made of men.

maneater

## AND I WONDER IF I LOVE THIS HARD
because i wonder if i'll ever be enough
if i will ever receive all that i put out
if i will ever receive all that i never had
if perhaps one day i'll feel held
if perhaps one day home wouldn't be so scary anymore
i wonder if i love this hard
because this is all i ever wanted
all i ever needed
and all i never had

jean-marie bub

and if you want the whole and
complete truth –

love was the only escape from the pain.
it gives me hope that someday

what i put out
will finally
be returned to me.

## ORANGES STREET BLUES

radiators hum,
reminding me that i am not alone. at least
that's what i tell myself
heat pushes through vents, howling under the moonlight that
slowly drips into my room

the leaves of my plants cascade down onto the floor,
surrounding the windows and its sill

i no longer feel stuck
i am filled with the life you stole from me.

my feet touch the cold, wooden floor
i am home.

blue is the warmest color.

jean-marie bub

**but who loves the poet?**

maneater

𝔜ou finished this book, which wasn't an easy thing to do. Affirm this to yourself, and know it to be true –

*I am fire I am glory I am gold*
*I hold power from the gods,*
*body mind & soul*

*I am not my trauma*
*I am not my body*
*I am not rebel without a cause*

*I am revolution*
*& rebellion & power & sin*

*I reclaim all that I thought I had lost,*
*& recognize it was just buried deep within.*

jean-marie bub

I love you
I love you
I love you
I love you
I love you
I love you
I love you
I love you
I love you
I love you
I love you
I love you
I love you
I love you
I love you
I love you
I love you

## self harm & recovery

recovery beings when you begin being honest — with what you feel, with what you need and with who you are. of course, it's easier said than done — but it's a journey worth embarking upon. recovery is waiting. always. no matter how invasive the darkness may be, there's always a light that lingers. whether this light is found through the vessel of a friend, a hobby such as writing or reading, or something as simple as the sunset — this light is always worth pursuing. is forward. there is no "falling back" after you decide you'd like to begin recovery. it's not linear. it's ok if all you've done today was survive. it's ok if you just made your bed. these are steps towards brighter days. this is progression — and it's different for everyone, but i urge you. please open up. to me. to a friend. to a stranger via hotline. to anyone. your story is worth telling and your voice needs to be heard. we can fight this together. just be honest and be you.
be resilient.
be brave.

recovery is worth pursuing. this is your sign.
you're going to be okay.

jean-marie bub

*my arms, 2019*

# help resources

if you need help, please speak with someone. there is no shame in needing someone to lean on.

Call the toll-free National Suicide Prevention Lifeline at 1-800-273-TALK (8255) to be connected with a trained counselor at a crisis center anytime.

text HOME to 741-741 to connect with a crisis counselor at the Crisis Text Line from anywhere in the U.S. It's free, 24/7, and confidential

If you're outside the United States, please visit iasp.info

If you have any questions, concerns or comments, feel free to DM me on Instagram @jeanmariebub, or email me at jeanmariebub@gmail.com

# maneater prompts

Use #MANEATERBYBUB when sharing, and when publishing, I ask that you please credit the prompt. Oh, and don't forget – tear his heart out.

1. What about you is weapon?
2. Write about yourself how you wish a significant other wrote about you. Realize you don't need anyone but you to discover your power. Bask in it.
3. Identify your power.
4. Identify your familiar.
5. Write an affirmation for your body.
6. Write an ode to your fourteen-year-old self. if you are fourteen... wait a few years and come back to this.
7. Cicadas under skin
8. What do your ancestors tell you in your dreams?
9. Athame
10. Venus
11. Fuck forgiving. Write an anti-forgiveness poem for them.
12. Write a letter to them and burn it. Take a picture of the letter on fire as the only thing to remember them by.
13. Tell me who and what you deserve.
14. Tell me how you want to be fucked.
15. Tell me how you become MANEATER.
16. Tell me how you reclaim your flesh.

17. Write a hex for them. But realize it's only writing – we don't hex what karma takes care of.
18. How would you plot your revenge?
19. Write from the perspective of your wound.
20. Who are you without your pain? Write it then live as that person. Post it on your mirror and read it everyday as affirmation.
21. Tell me how you plan on healing.
22. Promise yourself you'll flush the razors tonight. Keep the promise. Say your last words to them.
23. Name him/her/them. Publish or keep private. Do it for you.

Jean-Marie Bub (she/her) is an artist, author, survivor and activist living in Harlem who is dedicated to raising hell with her truth. On both paper and canvas, she puts emphasis on reclaiming one's body after experiencing abuse and sexual trauma.

Her work is aimed to legitimize women's anger, while holding space for survivors to undercover the feelings that become buried in rushed healing processes. She examines the guttural pain of womanhood, trauma, relationships and loss.

Her work has been featured in publications such as Pussy Magic, 'Reclaim: An Anthology of Women's Poetry,' No Tender Fences: an Anthology of Immigrant & First-Generation American poetry, Hellebore Magazine, and more. Her first book, Pulchritude and Soul, is featured in her high schools Mental Health curriculum.

maneater

# the maneater playlist

jean-marie bub

Made in the USA
Middletown, DE
13 February 2021